Philetus Walter Norris

The Calumet of the Coteau and Other Poetical Legends of the

Border

Philetus Walter Norris

The Calumet of the Coteau and Other Poetical Legends of the Border

ISBN/EAN: 9783337155971

Printed in Europe, USA, Canada, Australia, Japan

Cover: Foto ©Andreas Hilbeck / pixelio.de

More available books at **www.hansebooks.com**

THE CLIFF AND QUARRY OF THE PIPESTONE OR SACRED CALUMET.

THE

CALUMET OF THE COTEAU,

AND OTHER

POETICAL LEGENDS OF THE BORDER.

ALSO,

A GLOSSARY OF INDIAN NAMES, WORDS, AND WESTERN PROVINCIALISMS.

TOGETHER WITH

A GUIDE-BOOK

OF THE

YELLOWSTONE NATIONAL PARK.

By P. W. NORRIS,
FIVE YEARS SUPERINTENDENT OF THE YELLOWSTONE NATIONAL PARK.

PHILADELPHIA:
J. B. LIPPINCOTT & CO.
1883.

To my early and dear friend who long ago by the Miami of the Lakes, in the wilds of Northwestern Ohio, strengthened my youthful ambition, I am indebted for the impulses which from time to time found expression in poetic fancy.

As a reminder of those days, so fraught with pleasure and profit, and as a slight token of gratitude to one whose character I admire and whose friendship I cherish, the following legends are dedicated to the

HONORABLE MORRISON R. WAITE,
Chief Justice of the United States.

I SING IN SONGS.

I SING in songs of gliding lays
Of forest scenes in border days;
Of rippling rills in valleys green,
And mirrored hills in lakelet sheen;
Of mountain-peaks begirt with snow,
And flowery parks, pine-girt below;
Of daring deeds of border braves,
On dashing steeds, to gory graves;
Of brawny breast 'neath painted plume,
On warrior's crest, in dash to doom;
Of light canoe on dashing shore,
And daring crew, who'll row no more;
Of goblins grim and cañons grand,
And geysers spouting o'er the strand;
Of Mystic Lake, of Wonder-Land.

INTRODUCTION.

THE production of the stanzas which compose the following narratives of incidents, legends, and traditions of border-life are not the result of any preconceived plan or elaborate preparation, but are the spontaneous outgrowth of circumstances and events as diverse and peculiar as the strains in which they are written or the scenes which they portray.

Tender affection and filial regard for a disabled soldier sire of Pilgrim descent, an affectionate mother of Welsh birth and lineage, and a numerous family of young and dependent sisters, impelled my boyish footsteps from our frontier cabin of love to the toils and dangers of a trapper's life along the great lakes, rivers, and amid the mountains of the pathless Northwest, in order to assist one parent in his increasing age and failing strength, and the other in her efforts with the rude weaver's shuttle in providing for the comfort and education of my sisters. From this revered Welsh mother I doubtless inherit an ardent love for mountain and song. The stern realities of border-life strengthened the one and wellnigh strangled the other; and under the opinion, still retained, that the poet's fantastic visions rarely accord with the cool calculations requisite for business success, I seldom allowed these day-dreams encouragement or record. Yet these unbidden visions were occasionally pencilled by the camp-fire, in hours of danger, as a solace from care or as a tribute to the memory of cherished comrades gone; but they were seldom long retained amid my wanderings.

Those which memory cherished were published under the *nom de plume* of "Glen Alpine," my own name, for business reasons, being usually concealed.

Of these, "Gallant Charley Reynolds," "Cloud-Circled Mountains," and especially "The Union of the Valleys," published soon after the Custer massacre, were encouragingly received. Since that time the remaining poems have been written, usually with pencil only, when and where occasion called them forth, and preserved, which was generally all accorded them during my five successive years of arduous duties as superintendent of the Yellowstone National Park. Pending the adjustment of my accounts in connection with this duty, and the preparations for those of Ethnological research among the mounds and other prehistoric remains in the Mississippi Valley during the past season, these fugitive poems were gathered up, revised, and, with explanatory notes and a glossary, somewhat arranged, and now, together with a few additional legends, and a map and guide for the Yellowstone National Park, prepared for publication.

It must be evident that persons associating in youth with comrades of many nations, speaking dissimilar languages, the guttural jargon, or employing signs as a mode of communication, could hardly escape acquiring lasting habits of speech and a style of writing very unlike their native tongue; hence, despite change in the construction of verses, and the addition of connecting words in many of these stanzas, abundant evidence remains to prove they were written tinged with an idiom clearly distinct from ordinary English. This is regretted, and earnest efforts have been made for its modification in the recent use of words and construction of sentences. Thus the want of grammatical accuracy in this work is not as in those of some authors, an intentional provincialism, but the inherent defects of the early training of the author; and hence it is hoped that this consideration may somewhat turn aside the shafts of unfriendly criticism.

Perhaps it may be conceded that this admitted lack of style and finish in the verses is in part counterbalanced by the truthful description of the marvels in the Goblin and Wonder-Lands, and the ever-changing scenes of the border, in which the author has largely participated, and the faithful recital of the legends or traditions of the days agone.

Nor has the author sought to invade the sacred precincts of classic literature, or trespass upon the trodden fields of poetic fame, but as a tireless pioneer and pathfinder, he has explored the route, blazed the trail, and brought away, rough-hewn and unpolished, some of the countless gems hidden upon the rolling coteaus, the snow- and cliff-encircled parks and lovely valleys of an empire now in the closing throes of transition from a race of stoic lethargy to that of resistless energy and progress.

If, by the publication of these gliding narratives of slaughter, of sorrow, of heroism, or of hope, the author shall have rescued from impending oblivion a few of the thrilling scenes and unknown actors of this momentous era, and thereby encouraged others to fill future poetic volumes of authentic history, he will feel that recalling and publishing these camp-fire recollections and sketches of a life upon the border has not been utterly in vain.

TABLE OF CONTENTS.

	PAGE
THE CALUMET OF THE COTEAU	17
THE GOBLIN-LAND	40
THE MYSTIC LAKE OF WONDER-LAND	45
THE FAITHFUL LOVERS	50
GALLANT CHARLEY REYNOLDS	60
PILGRIMS OF THE YELLOWSTONE	63
CAPTIVE MAIDEN	67
THE WONDER-LAND	70
BOLD HERO OF THE BORDER	73
STALWART YEOMAN	75
GO WHERE DUTY CALLS THEE	77
THE DYING MANDANS	79
THE DYING TRAPPER	81
BOZEMAN BOLD	84
THE CLOUD-CIRCLED MOUNTAINS	86
WHERE ELSE ON EARTH?	88
BRADLEY THE BRAVE	90
FROM BIG-HORN'S BLEAK MOUNTAINS	92
MYSTIC LAND	94
THE GRANGER SONG	96
BORDER BRAVE	99
THE TATTOOED ARTIST	101
THE MOSQUITO	110
FRIGHTENED HANS	112
THE WINDING DELL	114
AFAR FROM THE CITIES AND HAMLETS OF MEN	117
OH, IS THERE IN THIS WORLD SO DREAR?	119
TO THE TIE AT HOME	121
THE WARRIOR'S GRAVE	123
I SING IN SONGS	125

TABLE OF CONTENTS.

	PAGE
BLAZE BRIGHTLY, O CAMP-FIRE!	127
UNION OF THE VALLEYS	129
OH, FOR BARD TO TRULY TREASURE	131
RUSTIC BRIDGE AND CRYSTAL FALLS	132
HIGH TOWERS THE CRAGGY SUMMIT	135
LONELY GLEN	137
REYNOLDS'S DIRGE	138
YES, BE IT THUS	139
IN CABIN, CAMP, OR COUNCIL	140
YES, EVERY ONE A MAN	141
THE ARTIST STANLEY	145
MIN-NE-HA-HA	146
LOVELY RIVER	147
BURIAL TEEPEE	148
BOLD TRAPPER OF THE CAMP-FIRE	149
THE WARRIOR'S DIRGE	150
CYPRESS SHADOWS	152
I'VE TRAILED THE PROUD COLUMBIA	153
HO, WAKEN!	157
NORTHERN CLIME	159
DE SOTO	162
NOTES	171
GLOSSARY	223
GUIDE-BOOK OF THE YELLOWSTONE NATIONAL PARK	235

LIST OF ILLUSTRATIONS.

		PAGE
1.	The Cliff and Quarry of the Pipestone or Sacred Calumet	*Frontispiece.*
2.	The Indian Council	24
3.	Custer's Battle-ground	37
4.	The Goblin Labyrinths	43
5.	The Daring Maiden	56
6.	The Dying Trapper	82
7.	Rustic Bridge and Crystal Falls	133
8.	Map of the Yellowstone National Park	235
9.	Mammoth Hot Springs	245
10.	Map of the Upper Geyser Basin	255
11.	Bee-Hive Geyser	257

THE CAL-U-MET OF THE COTEAU.

¹ SAY, hast thou seen the cal-u-met* of pink or purple bright,
A pipe-bowl in the council, a hatchet in the fight?
And heard the Indian legend, all of a deluge grand,
Of time agone uncounted o'er the Da-ko-ta land;
When a remnant of the red men upon a rocky crest
Were gathered where the eagle had built his lofty nest,
And the rising waters swallowed all save a virgin lone,
Who clung to the war-eagle and nestled in his home;
When from receding waters the rocky crest arose,
Lo! turned to shining jasper were mingled friends and foes?

Then hovered the Man-i-tou† to view the horrid scene,
A cliff of rocky warriors above the coteau green:
"This rock," he cries, "is sacred; no warrior here shall stand
With bended bow and arrow, or battle-lance in hand;
No war-whoop here shall echo, no scalping-knife shall gleam,
But o'er the rolling coteau shall glide a crystal stream,
And emerald pools shall sparkle along the lovely vale,
For cleansing baths of warriors, where foes shall not assail;

---

* Cal'u-mèt, the sacred pipe of peace.
† Man-*i* (pronounced *è*) -tou, the Mysterious Spirit, or God.

But all shall meet in friendship around the rocky crest,
Where the weak shall dwell in safety and the 'weary be at rest.' "

Thus spake the proud Man-i-tou unto the mongrel brood
Of the maiden and war-eagle, who stern around him stood,
Who on the crest an altar of shining jasper made,
And sacrifice of bison upon it reeking laid,
As pledge of compact sacred, when, lo ! from cal'met-bowl—
The wand of the Man-i-tou—the flames of heaven roll
From the stem to waiting altar, as lightning from above,
And incense sweet from bison seals pledge of peace and love,—
From altar, then, Man-i-tou quick carves a cal'met bright,
And how to smoke it taught them, then vanished from their sight ;
But the Was-sa-mo-win* flashing transpierced the eagle's nest,
And glazed to hardest adamant the towering jasper crest ;
But the foot-print of the eagle deep in the rock remains,
And the blood of slaughtered bison the crag a crimson stains.

Forth went the stalwart red men, and wandered o'er the earth,
Each clan with purple cal'mets carved at their place of birth,
To smoke on each occasion of council for a peace,
When all who smoked to totem pledged massacre should cease ;

---

* Was'sa-mo'win, lightning.

But the pipe with blade of hatchet, and stem with eagle's plume,
And paint of bright vermilion, are smoked as call of doom !
For eagle's plume on hatchet-stem was the totem of the sire,
Which warriors made in battle, and stoics in the fire ;
While the bowl of peaceful maiden was smoked for war to cease,
That each should meet as kindred, and all should dwell in peace.

But lost were maidens' cal-u-mets, while the warrior's hatchet new
Was ever carved more gorgeous, as savage habits grew ;
And, as virtue ever suffers by compromise with crime,
So the eagle's bloody hatchet hewed the maiden's pipe in time ;
And when her children wandered far to the cal'met land,
Lo ! too hard was rock to make them with tool in human hand ;
In sore distress, the Wa-kon, as mother of the race,
With sacrifice and prayer, was sought to show her face ;
When lo ! in cloud she hovered above the eagle's nest,
And sweet-voiced like the zephyrs, her children thus addressed :

" Oh, children ! my children ! your prayers I hear,
Go forth on the coteau and gather the deer,
The elk and the bison, and antelope fleet,
For slaughter and offering as sacrifice sweet ;
[2] But the bison, so lofty, so fleet, and so white,
Oh ! mar not his beauty, but follow his flight !

Where his hoofs turn the rocks on the trail of the slain,
In that crimson-stained rill seek for pipe-stone again,—
Carve and smoke from the quarry by blood rendered soft;
Live in peace with each other,—I'll view from aloft!
That the eagle may sanction this compact divine,
[3] These five eggs I leave for your witness and mine;
[4] Lo! beneath are two grottos for Wa-root-ka's home,
To watch all your doings wherever I roam.
Farewell, my dear children! I'm goddess at home;
But the proud eagle governs the warriors who roam!"

Thus spake the mother Wa-kon, beneath her floating hair
Of waving spray and rainbow, then vanished into air.
Adown into the valley they trailed the bison white,
When near the eggs (now adamant) beheld a cheering sight;
Of cal'met rock a fragment by bison hoof upturned,
In stream of blood from sacrifice, upon the coteau burned;
The quarry found, deep in the ground, beside the crystal stream,
Ever retains those crimson stains, matchless to carve and gleam;
Whence alone have cal'mets purple for all the Indian race
Quarried been beneath the waters, which bear a crimson trace.

Full soon were pilgrims gathered, from Win-ne-ba-go band,
And Cher-o-kee and Choc-taw, from sunny southern land;
The Mo-hawk and Wy-an-dotte, from eastern timbered vales,
Brule, Flat-head, and Wa-lu-la, amid the western dales;
The Sem-i-nole and Eu-taw, 'mid creeping southern vines,
Bold Chip-pe-wa and Hu-ron, from tow'ring northern pines;

THE CAL-U-MET OF THE COTEAU. 21

The Pe-quod and Mo-hic-an, from Atlantic's granite shore,
With Cay-use and Nis-qual-la, from the loud Pacific's roar;
The Ban-nock and Sho-shon-e, dull Ute and crafty Crow,
⁵ Bold Chey-enne and Da-ko-ta, the latter called Si-oux.

Brave Paw-nee of the prairies, Pi-ute from Lava Plains,
A-rick-a-ree and Man-dan (whose fields Missouri drains);
Pilgrims from each were gathered, friends here, though elsewhere foes!
In pools removed was war-paint, plunged hatchets, lance, and bows,
As brothers all united to gather, carve, and smoke
Cal-u-mets from quarry sacred, and Man-i-tou's love invoke;
Young warriors with ambition the "Leaping-Rock" to press,
Found horrid death in failure, and honor in success;
⁶ In jasper cairn they buried the maid and warrior gone,
And bright their totems painted upon the walls of stone.

O, lovely days of beauty and happy nights of peace!
All countless are the bison, the elk are slain with ease;
The Man-dan round his earth-lodge his garden tills secure,
The yellow trout, and speckled, fill dashing streamlet pure;
⁷ The woolly-sheep and big-horn skip near the crests of snow,
Unnumbered in the valleys are the shaggy buffalo;
Swift antelope and black-tails bedeck the treeless plains,
And swans with snowy plumage the glades Missouri drains;
In light canoes the Chip-pe-was their Mon-o-nim* secure,
These countless gifts of providence to nature's God allure.

---

* Mon-o-nim, wild rice.

Oh, these blissful days are waning, and bitter days begun,
With the coming of the pale-face athwart the rising sun !
Their "big canoes" with eagle-wings are matchless in
   the race,
Terrific are the warriors with bearded throat and face,
⁸ Bestride fleet hornless bison, resistless in the strife,
And from their side oft flashes a long and flaming knife ;
From bosom gleams bright totems, war-bonnets shield
   their eyes,
Each war-lance darting lightning, their thunders rend
   the skies ;
Flames from their monster cal-u-mets blaze like a meteor
   star,
And unseen barbless arrows are deadly from afar.

The artless child of nature in silent wonder gazed,
⁹ Then from the "Mighty Medicine" in terror fled amazed.
Scarce had these tales of wonder traversed the mighty
   lakes,
Ere echoing new thunder, primeval silence breaks ;
Nor hissing bolts of murder pursue for human gore,
¹⁰ Pure Hen-ne-pin and Du-luth visit for good the shore ;
And through untrodden forests they seek the boundless
   West,
¹¹ Till the Prairie Min-ne-tan-ka their wanderings arrest,
When lo ! amid the pastures of mingled flowers and
   green,
High o'er the Min-ne-ha-ha, St. Anthony is seen.
On halo crest of rainbow that spans his cañon walls
He with his own name christens the Mis-sis-sip-pi Falls,
And hails the wond'ring Frenchman, in accents clear
   and strong,
"Adown this mighty river in safety glide along

THE CAL-U-MET OF THE COTEAU. 23

From the lake-land of the pine-tree to the cypress by the sea,
But along its western borders are a people brave and free.
No pale-face foot in sacrilege may press Dakota's plains,
For thus our Wa-kan-tan-ka the sacred right ordains.
With curling smoke of cal-u-met they'll greet you to their shore,
But all advance the tomahawk will terminate in gore."
With kind intent the warning given, in birchen-bark canoe,
Like Chippewa, St. Anthony quick vanishes from view.

Full soon the sons of nature in mighty council meet,
To pledge the roving pale-face as brother all to greet.
¹²With purple pipe the chieftain first heavenward points above,
Then east, and west, and north, and south, for witnesses to prove
The friendship that he proffers, upward with curling smoke,
Prove ever true and lasting, or the Wa-kon's curse invoke!
With one long puff from sacred pipe, each passes it along,
'Mid bold harangues of warriors and mingled dance and song,
Till all have pledged Man-i-tou each as a friend to know,
While sun and moon shall circle, or crystal waters flow.

Thus, where the Min-ne-so-ta the Mis-sis-sip-pi meets,
And fairy Min-ne-ha-ha in matchless beauty sleeps,
Warriors of Man-i-to-ba and from Mis-sou-ri's strand,
Foxes of Mil-wau-kee and the Mi-am-i grand,
Chieftain of Min-ne-o-la, on crested helmet sheen,
Runners of Min-ne-o-pa, from rolling coteaus green,
With fiery Mish-e-wau-kee pledged the Man-i-tou God
That coteaus of Da-ko-ta by whites should ne'er be trod;

24   THE CAL-U-MET OF THE COTEAU.

But the roaring Min-ne-tan-ka a border hence shall be
Betwixt the native rovers and those from o'er the sea.
First pale-face then from the council adown the river
   passed;
By the fate of Indian nations, happy had they been the
   last!

THE INDIAN COUNCIL.

Too soon, alas! the Long-Knife upon his charger came;
Anew they smoked the cal'met, and friendship pledged
   again;
But no Le Sueur or Jo-li-ette, with hearts of truth and
   love:
'Twas now a band of traders, robbers where'er they rove.

With honeyed words, but hearts of lust, they promised
    but to win,
Practised vile arts on innocence, proud revelling in sin;
Cheating alike in what they bought, and gaudy trinkets
    sold;
Every craft was justified to garner furs and gold;
The flowing cup of sorrow they luring hold in sight,—
Pelf sanctifies the weapons,—" success is ever right."
[13] Naught care they for the sufferings, the hunger, thirst, or
    cold
Of agonizing victims, so with gore they gather gold.

At first they taste with caution, then drink and drink
    again,
Like flock of simple goslings, soon sense with bottle
    drain;
Then dance, and laugh, and swagger,—men, not maid-
    ens, kiss, then fight.
Reeling, they fall while boasting; for, to act the demon
    right,
Needless stage, or school, or college; for lo! one bottle
    full
Of liquid fire ruin brings to wisdom, wealth, and soul,
Slaying alike all nations,—the merry sons of France,
The sturdy sons of Erin, or Brule with scalping dance.
Proud slaves it makes of votaries, who freedom ne'er re-
    gain,—
The viler gall the fetters, the sweeter seems the chain.

Thus with the simple red men: entranced by poison vile,
While to their old friends cruel, they on the traders smile,
And in their revels barter, not furs and health alone,
But wife and daughter's virtue, to trader, viler grown.
And when the coteau-mother, her simple race to save,
Invokes the Eagle chieftain, him too she finds a slave

Of passion vile and cruel—oh, horrid tale to tell!—
His daughter, young and lovely, to trader seeks to sell,
¹⁴"For wife to grace the harem, and firm unite his race
With chieftain of the Long-Knife and smiling bearded
   face!

Behold the mother Wa-kon, upon the coteau crest,
In agony imploring for her people sore oppressed:
   "Man-i-tou! oh, Man-i-tou! save us
   From the foe that would enslave us;
   From the pale-face ever smiling
   On the maiden he's beguiling,
   And from ancient brave confiding,
   Robs the pinto he's bestriding,
   To the warrior proud and daring
   Cup of Min-ne-bo-ta bearing,
   Thus the fount of sorrow nursing,
   Soon a flood of crime and cursing!

   "Now, my chief, once true and loving,
   From my arms is ever roving,
   And for fount of fiery water
   Seeks to barter darling daughter;
   Oh, night of woe, and morn of sorrow,
   Dark the day and drear the morrow!
   Oh, my stricken form is quaking,
   And my yearning heart is breaking!
   Oh, Man-i-tou! save my daughter,
   And chief and race from crime and slaughter!"

Where the lovely Mississippi unites with Pepin Lake
¹⁵Tower high o'er crystal waters huge crags of crumbling
   slate;

In fairy grove, 'mid prairie,—hard by,—stood pale-face
    den,
And there pure Min-ne-ha-ha was to have wedded been;
But ere she left the fairy falls which honor still her name,
She to her Min-ne-o-la pledged faithful to remain;
Then down the stream in birch canoe he vanishes unseen
To Pepin's hidden grotto, and there awaits his queen;
With life and hope and nimble step, if fate allow her to,
If not, to leap from towering rock, and die with lover true.

The spirit of the Eagle, with hatchet, plume, and lance,
Was ever for the war-path, the reeking scalp, and dance,
While the nature of the maiden through all these ages ran
With tenderness to woman and fellowship with man.
Tho' wars were fierce and bloody upon the distant plain,
O'er all the sacred coteau there spouts no crimson stain,—
And in its vale of refuge beneath the rocky dome
Are ever peace and safety as in a parent's home;
But red men on the river have evil grown apace,—
The doings of the Long-Knife have ever cursed the race.

The trader's speckled harem of every tribe and hue,
Of wrangling whelps and pappoose, and maidens ever new,
'Twas there pure Min-ne-ha-ha was sought for a queen
    awhile,
[16] Then thrust aside degraded, to delve in kennel vile!
Strange if with such example she fails to see the snare,
Or seeing, preferred dying; but first a maiden's prayer:
"Man-i-tou! oh, Man-i-tou! grant hunger, thirst, and
    toil,
Faint, paddling in the rapids or delving in the soil,
Share the sufferings of our people, the perils of our race,
But wed me not to pale-face,—pray spare me that dis-
    grace,—

I love my Min-ne-o-la,—oh! let me share his lot,
Or deep beneath the waters be evermore forgot!"

But frenzied was the Eagle by venom from the still,
And to gratify that passion relentless was his will;
In vain was mother's pleading, unheeded maiden's prayer,
His warriors' scowls derided ('twas in the trader's lair);
With hatchet high uplifted (no passage knew to plain),
Vowed she should Long-Knife marry, or mingle with the
    slain!
The daring wife of Eagle, with all a mother's love,
[17] The secret passage opens,—quick darts the turtle-dove!

"Love, mother,—oh, my mother! to you and chieftain
    true,
Pure, I'll die with Min-ne-o-la!" and to the crest she
    flew,—
No frenzied sire nor Long-Knife, nor lance nor quivering
    dart,
Can reach the flying maiden or pierce the fluttering heart.
The summit gained, alas! one glance at earth, then heaven!
Then from the giddy crest she leaped, like bolt by thunder
    riven,
Deep 'mid the crystal waters, pure as her truth and love,
To arms of waiting chieftain, where mermaids ever rove!
Though ages long have vanished, warriors and nations
    sleep,
[18] Still oft in wave-kissed grottos sing they at "Maiden's
    Leap."

"All hidden our grotto beneath the blue waters,
  That requiems murmur as gliding along;
Nor wrath of the Eagle at queen of his daughters
  Our refuge shall darken, or fetter our song:

O Wa-kon ! our mother, dost spirit still hover
   Around the bold cliffs and blue waters below,
While evening's soft zephyrs waft low wails of lover
   O'er Pepin's pure waters at twilight aglow ?
And while Min-ne-so-ta meanders in sadness,
   Low, murmuring through valley, 'adieu to our race.'

[19] And thou, Mis-sis-sip-pi, bear'st temples in gladness,
   With loud strains of music their progress to trace,
Shall plumed Min-ne-o-la, unchanging as lover,
   With paddle scarce dipping, chant boat-song of braves,
And pure Min-ne-ha-ha, the wild cliffs above her,
   Make laughing re-echo, our dirge from the waves !"

Not humbled by his folly, nor by its woe and cost,
But furious at the mother whose love the maiden lost,
He sealed with warrior's hatchet the cal'met Wa-kon's
   doom !
Too late drunken Man-i-tou pales 'neath his paint and
   plume,
The stroke his race has destined, tho' struggling to re-
   main,
Yet sure to fade and vanish. Once in a sober vein,
Proud Eagle pleads in anguish,—no Wa-kon hears his
   calls:
No more remorse, but bitterness henceforth his mind
   enthralls,—
The mercy of the maiden has fled the copper race,—
The vengeance of the Eagle, relentless, takes its place !

And now, alas ! the Eagle in anger chose a mate,—
Not one who fosters mercy, but ever favors hate ;
Who like an earthly vixen with jealousy oppressed,
Quick soar'd to cal'met coteau, and rent the Eagle's nest ;

Then perched upon the eminence, to cool her wrath awhile,
But nursing roused it higher, with purposes most vile:
"This is the Eagle's heritage, and I his favored mate,
These, Wa-kon's loving children, their every act I hate;
They meet and wash the war-paint in my crystal bathing-pools,
They dig and smoke in friendship, and act like simple fools;
As tho' our elk and bison were made for them alone,
They sing and dance and gabble, wild revelling in our home,
And plotting with each other against their royal chief,
That *I* am an intruder, *War-Eagle* but a thief!
While they audacious plunder the pillars of our throne,
And whittle smoking cal-u-mets from our choicest purple stone;
I'll teach them how to chatter, to frolic, sing, and dance,—
These children of another,—oh, how I'll make them prance!"

Then to the Eagle hastens, near Min-ne-o-la's home,
(Lest her untimely absence allow her chief to roam);
Like a true stepmother, his willing ear she fills
With projects grand but simple, to 'scape all earthly ills.
'Twas but to borrow thunder, and lance and gleaming knife,
And steeds of Shun-ka-wa-kan,* and follow their new life
Of ease upon the prairies, at cal'met coteau bright,
Demanding of these pilgrims by what heritage or right

---

* Shun-ka-wa-kan, sacred dog,—*i.e.*, horse.

They live in ease and plenty on our deer and antelope,
And dig away our quarry, or lazily to mope,
While we from home as strangers wander,—"Oh, my chief,
Would thou wert Eagle warrior, then were our sorrows brief!"

    "Hold, my consort!" cries the Eagle,
      "Have all as you will;
    I am ready, I am willing,—
      Revel, rob, and kill.
[20] Bury purple cal'met peaceful;
      Quench its azure smoke;
    Grasp the hatchet crimson reeking,
      Death at every stroke!

    When the simple peaceful pilgrim
      Seeks a cal'met bright,
    I will burnish, I will furnish
      For a wampum bright.
    I will slaughter on the coteau
      Till a crimson stream
    Floods the quarry, drowns the pilgrim,
      And I crown my queen.
    Then will follow Min-ne-ke-wa,
      Long a trail of gore,
    From the coteau to the river
      And Lake Pepin's shore!"

Thus a new era opens,—once his passions roused
By wine and crafty woman, he with the pale-face housed
Hostage ample in payment for the murderous tools of war;
Then hastens in wild splendor to the coteau of the fair.

The pilgrims in amazement gather along the stream
To view the prancing chargers and of arms the burnished
   gleam ;
Nor long were left to wonder, for loud the trumpet calls,
And musket peals re-echo along the rocky walls,
Above the roaring waters, beside the Leaping-Rock,
Which quivers like an aspen from the unwonted shock !

Soon the War-Eagle summons unto his teepee all
(While, Satan-like, his consort prompts menace with the
   call) :
"Why sap ye the foundation of my rocky home and nest,
By digging for the cal'met beneath its tottering crest ?
A tribute's mine,—a portion of what you quarry here ;
One-half of all your cal-u-mets,—sure, that is not too dear ;
Beside, of deer and bison and beaver of the rill
Mine be the furs and robes,—of the carcass eat your fill,
Save choice of loin tender,—hence pledged to me and
   mine,
As coteau's great Wa-kan-da, by a standing right divine."

In blank and mute amazement the pilgrims stand around,
Like claims of crafty rulers people wiser oft astound ;
Full soon they break and scatter, departing each his way,
The cowards to pay tribute, the bold the chief to slay.
But vain on earth is innocence, the weak against the
   strong,
For "might makes right," and hopelessly fights right
   against the wrong.
Full soon from cowards' tribute, or plunder stained with
   gore,
The ghoul is paid, with usury, and shrewdly trusted more ;
For slaves of vice and rapine are often from this cause
By masters safer trusted than those obeying laws.

²¹ Thus soon the Wạ-kan-she-cha had crushed or slain the race
Of the ever-loving Wa-kon, and a covey reared in place—
Fit whelps of the War-Eagle and his Cay-ou-ta mate—
As venomous as serpents, as sly and sure as fate ;
In league with vilest pale-face, and through him with the de'il,
By courage, or through cunning, make all their neighbors feel
That such a race of robbers resistless soon must prove,
And slaughtered are, commingled, or far away remove ;
Thus all winds seemed to favor the fierce Da-ko-ta clan,
Scoffers at the laws of God ! deriders of the rights of man !

With the cunning of Mahomet, a religion new they made,
To suit their lust and rapine, deeming war a holy trade ;
Each Sioux born a warrior, the steed his constant friend,
His earliest hope the sun-dance, to nerve and courage blend ;
Thence proudly on the war-trail, a reeking proof to claim,
Scalps helpless squaw or pappoose (all count a coup the same),
Then yelling to the council, bedaubed with sickening gore,
Flaunts maiden's scalp as warrior,—then hastens after more ;
Each thought and plan and struggle is for a warrior's fame,
Blood-daubed and painted savage, loud glorying in his shame ;
Sure if his fate in battle be from his steed to die,
In bliss to soon bestride him, with plume on bonnet high !

Thus the courage of the eagle and the cunning of the wolf
Are blended in the Sioux, in their very web and woof;
c

A score of clans they scatter far o'er the western plains,
From the lovely mountain valleys to the glades Missouri
   drains,
Build their teepees far in Britain and their lodges 'long
   the Platte,
While professing peace and friendship ravage like the
   mountain-cat;
With deep regret the chieftain gathers his clan, to know
The guilty,—all are innocent,—"Sure," says the culprit,
   "'twas the Crow."
With outward grief but secret sneer at pale-face want of
   sense,
Rations and arms they thus secure ("poor lambs!") for
   self-defence!

Then, basely, from the council, they revel as of old,
In slaughter of the ranch-men, and pilgrim seeking gold;
The Crow and the Shoshone, and the treaty still sustain,
As firmly binding others, while they its terms disdain;
Their gorgeous tents and teepees loom grander every day;
With reservation plunder, or from murder on the way,—
To lairs beyond the prairies, far o'er the sterile plains,
Amid the rolling coteaus the mighty Big-Horn drains,
Along a smiling valley beneath a rocky crest,
Where Sioux squaw and warrior in teepees seemed at rest;
When Custer from the Rose-Bud, adown a streamlet came,
Not scouting well for ambush, but boldly seeking fame,
And rashly scattering warriors, which united were too few,
Charged fearless 'mid the teepees where leaden arrows
   flew.
Grim smiled the taurine chieftain, as the war-whoop in
   the vale
Shrill, knelled the fate of Custer, and his country left to
   wail!

Oh, chosen lair of ambush! oh, fatal charge of braves!
No mercy for the living, and for the dead no graves!
For vain were deeds of daring, 'mid countless hosts of foes
Commingled in the torrent which red with carnage flows,—
Or on the coteau struggling for victory or retreat,
With sword and carbine opening a route through pintos
   fleet,—
'Mid lasso, lance, and hatchet, the conflict soon is o'er,
In slaughter of our vet'rans who foe shall meet no more!
And when the evening shadows would hide the scene of
   shame,
Bright gleams the knife and hatchet by blazing teepee's
   flame;
And fiends with reeking trophies, each marred with bloody
   stain,
Arrayed in gory garments and tresses of the slain,
With shout and strut and swagger and screeching ambush
   yell,
Mimic the groans of dying, on scenes of scalping dwell,
Till hungry ghouls grow eager, and venom, conquering
   age,
Joins plumed and plumeless savages in revelry and rage,—
Each boasting of his glory in daring days of yore,—
While painting for the war-trail fresh butchery and gore.

And now from our legend a moment refrain,
In this valley to linger o'er dust of the slain,
[22] And 'mid the wild roses with carnage once red,
Oh! chant for our heroes the "Dirge of the Dead,"—
These heroes whose duties were finished too soon,
Rosy morning of promise beclouded ere noon;
When the steed and his rider vain struggled for shore
At the ford, where the torrent ran purple with gore;

From that dark cloud of battle, red field of the slain,
Sad tidings reach kindred, fond hoping in vain;
May each mourning parent thank God for a son,
Whose troth to his country is faithfully done!
[23] On the crest of the coteau once crimson with gore,
Oh, gather our heroes! their battles are o'er,
And the "long roll and rally" shall rouse them no more!

Soft zephyrs sweet whisper their sighs o'er the plain;
" Revered by our country, not fallen in vain,
Though moulder our ashes and lowly each bed,
'Tis only life's casket which sleeps with the dead;
Our spirits are basking afar from the grave,
In bowers of Eden awaiting the brave,
Where the warrior with hatchet ne'er enters for gore;
For cal'mets of purple are smoked as of yore,
With friends and with comrades in bliss evermore.

When from such feast these demons, begrimed with paint
    and gore,
Leave wolves to finish revel, and hasten after more;
[24] Nor bold as men of courage 'gainst remnant on the hill,
But prowling 'long the border, the innocent to kill;
As vultures scent the carrion, each teepee of the brood
Along the trail to slaughter swarms forth its whelps of
    blood!
The bold, thrifty yeoman seeks wealth in the West,
The mate of his bosom a dove from its nest;
Through deserts and dangers they suffer and roam,
Till in sweet sheltered valley they make them a home;
Soon neighbors build round them, all labor in peace,
Till of strength over-conscious does vigilance cease.

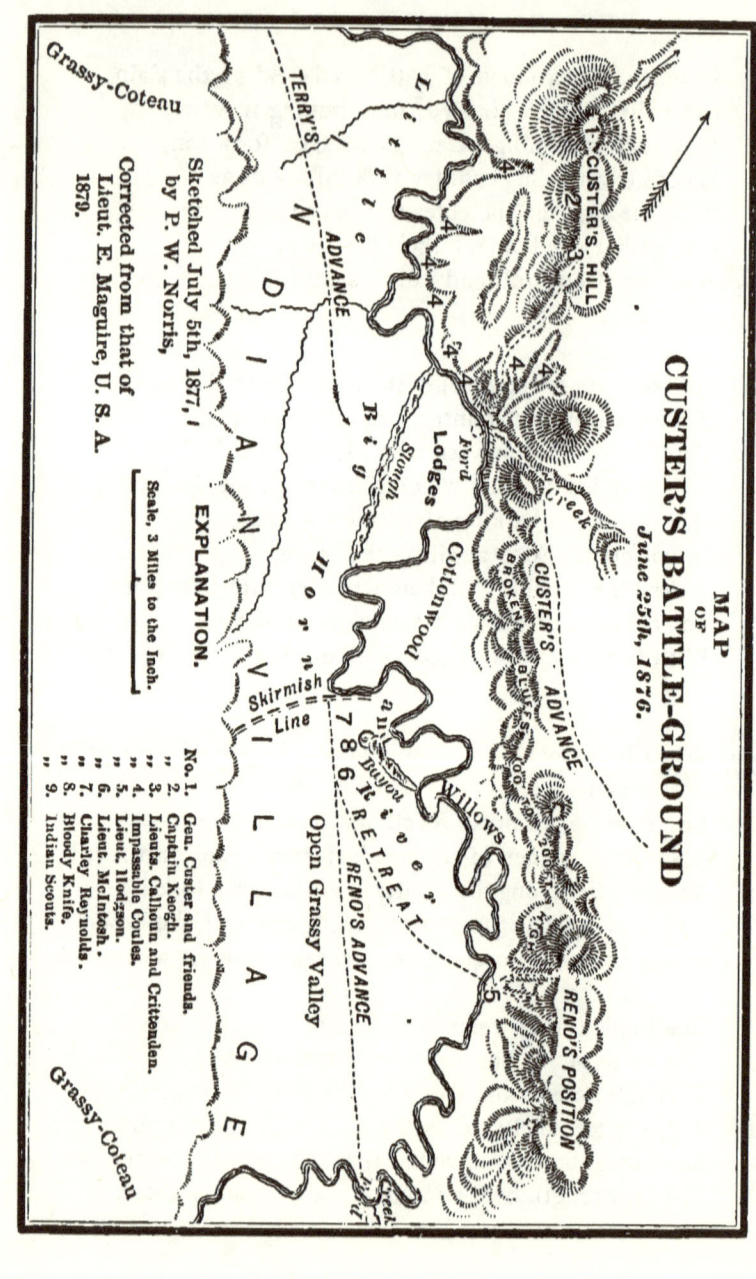

THE CAL-U-MET OF THE COTEAU.

Bestride his fleet pinto, over mountain and glen,
Rides the proud Sioux chieftain unto rapine again,
With ghouls from the slaughter of our Custer and men,
And whelps from their kennels in each valley and glen,
From the crests of the mountains white glist'ning in snow,
These friends scan this Eden all-enchanting below;
In darkness descending,—fitting season of crime,—
While the orb of the evening refuses to shine,
Like the scream of the eagle o'er the nest of the dove
Is the war-whoop of savage in the valley of love;
Like true painted demons, naught is sacred they find,—
Happy homes are before them, smoking ruins behind.

But the sword of vengeance tardy, erst gleaming o'er the brood
Of the Eagle and Cay-ou-ta, must now be drenched in blood
Drawn forth for that of pilgrims upon the coteau slain,—
Mercy's plea from innocence, be now as then in vain.
From the coteaus of Wy-o-ming and Co-lo-ra-do's plains
To Sas-ka-sha-an foaming, that Britain's forest drains;
[25] From the fairy Min-ne-ha-ha and lover's wailing strand
To snowy mountains tow'ring athwart the Wonder-Land,
Revel their Indian neighbors; none their fate bemoan;
The children reap the harvest by cruel parents sown.
In gory banquet reeking sinks warrior, maid, and child,
'Mid blazing tents and teepees, by revelry defiled;
Swells one loud wail of agony from sea of flame and gore,
Like scream of dying eagle, then silence evermore!

Long the spirit of the Wa-kon fond hovered o'er her race,
Then from a land of horrors she eastward turns her face,
To view on sacred coteau the cal-u-met smoked again
In happy homes of comfort, 'mid golden fields of grain.

The dwellers there a people, though pale-face to the view,
In love and kindness living, oh, cheering vision new!
High soaring, long she views them: "oh, happy people blest,
Who mingle love and valor, anew I'll build my nest,
And in memory of War-Eagle, as in the days of old,
Ere by Min-ne-wa-kan captured and to the Long-Knife sold,
[26] On the banners of this people let his pinions soar above
With my maiden's cap of Justice, of Liberty, and Love!"

THE GOBLIN-LAND.

OH, know ye the legend, when waves of the sea
Deep rolled o'er the summits of mountains to be,
Which slowly but surely upheaved from below,
Rose taller and broader, till crested with snow,
And bubble-like bursting in throes to go higher,
Were sheeted in lava, in sulphur and fire?
And fierce was the conflict, and fearful the roar
Of cold lashing surf on a seething hot shore,
Charge of seas on a land they should swallow no more.

Long, long roll the ages, and cold the cliffs grow,
Cloud-hidden their summits, grove-dotted below;
Wear prairies and coteaus bright carpets of green,
And streamlets enchanting meander between;
And forests majestic, and vine-trellised bowers,
Fringe glens as of Eden, all brilliant with flowers,
With roses and daisies, and pale elenore,
Whose nectar the honey-bees gather in store
For banquets of gods when the summer is o'er.

There finny forms sparkle like gems in the rills,
And elk with broad antlers proud stalk o'er the hills;
The goat and the big-horn high trail in the snow,
The deer and the bison in green vales below;
The black eagle soars round the pinnacle high
Till a wild lamb perceiving, as a bolt from the sky,
In his talons quick bears him for a feast in the glade,

Near the lion low crouching, whose dinner is made
Of victor and victim, in tanglewood shade.

In broad slimy marshes leviathans roar,
And mermaids are combing their locks by the shore;
Full deep in green waters the coral reefs form,
Till palm-shaded islets defy the wild storm;
And sharks, ever famished and eager for prey,
Devour with their victims the monsters who slay;
While o'er the broad ocean the albatross sails,
'Mid porpoise and dolphins and loud-spouting whales,
And sea-birds, foam-skimming, exult in the gales.

²⁹ Then man, hairy giant, strode forth in his might,
Erect like his Maker, with knowledge of right;
Inventor of weapons, first builder of fire,
Lone trader of trophies, with soul to soar higher;
Loin-girded, else naked, majestic in form,
With mate and their offspring cave-sheltered from storm;
Terrific his combats with lion and bear,
For food and for shelter, in glen or in lair;
But tusk, claw, and talons, and instincts are vain
'Gainst man and his weapons, on ocean or plain;
For man, as his birthright, was destined to reign.

Ages on ages have circled and fled,
And countless the heroes who sleep with the dead;
Earth teems with the millions unnumbered of men;
Fish, beasts, birds, and reptiles crowd sea, sky, and glen;
But man is polluted, and woman is vile,
With beasts, birds, and serpents commingling in guile;
And monsters all hideous, in form and in lust,
Stalk forth in the forests, or crawl in the dust,—
Earth is ripe for God's vengeance of fire 'neath its crust.

As evening's low murmurs from storm-cloud afar
Grow louder, till thunder the heavens ajar,
So moanings, half-smothered, in womb of the Earth,
In wailing and trembling, like travail of birth,
Grow louder and fiercer, till the thin crust is rent,
And lava all seething in billows finds vent.
In vain guilty mortals their revels bewail ;
Too late,—prayers for mercy are waft on the gale ;
Unheeded the howling of monsters in pain ;
God's vengeance, outpouring, rolls over the plain !
Like harlots of Sodom, all revelled in sin,
Gomorrahs of brimstone are walling them in ;
Commingled in matrix of slime, which encase
30 Men, mermaids, and monsters, each sphinx-like in place,
And mountains hurled o'er them, from Heaven hides trace.

Unnumbered the circles of sun and of stars ;
Terrific the earthquakes, and fearful their scars ;
And tempests, fierce howling, of hail and of snow,
And frosts, all eroding, hurl fragments below,
Unearthing each monster, each reptile and beast,
Nude vixen and warrior gigantic, at feast,
Where guests are stone-visaged, all lifeless and cold ;
Side-dishes, shell-fossils, as glistening as gold,
And viands, charred remnants of comrades of old.

Still deeper eroded the labyrinths grow,
And taller the Goblins, with helmets of snow.
Proud o'er them the eagle, with undazzled eye,
Scans sheep on the snow-fields, then swoops from the sky ;
The goat and the big-horn there covert oft finds
In archways of grottos, where the moaning of winds

THE GOBLIN LABYRINTHS.

Are requiems chanting, sharp, changing, and low,
Of Hoodoos unearthly 'mid the lava's o'erflow.
[31] And men of the mountains, of Sheep-Eater band,
Of game and of plunder make sacrifice grand
To monster stone-gods in the weird "Goblin-Land."

THE MYSTIC LAKE OF WONDER-LAND.

I SING of lake, of rippling rills,
Of sunny streams from snowy hills;
Of hissing pools with sulphur tide,
In gulches deeper far than wide;
Of foaming falls in cañon grand,
The Mystic Lake of Wonder-Land.

For here, begirt with mountain-chains,
Snow-clad mist-clouds hide grassy plains;
'Mid terraced slopes, pine-clad and green,
Reflected bright on emerald sheen,
Of bosom thine, 'neath turret high,
Bright-blending water, earth, and sky.

Thus seen in quiet summer's eve,
Eden it seems with naught to grieve;
But howling storms and piercing wails
Come with autumnal frosts and gales;
32 And chilling blasts resistless come
Adown thy fingers, palm, and thumb.

Oh, have I not in trying hour,
In craft too frail bewailed thy power?
With bending mast and rending sail,
And dashing wave o'er icy rail,
And foaming surf on rocky strand,
To shores of ice on mystic hand?

Oh, night of horrors! on that shore,
When fire and surf discordant roar,
And timber, tempest-reft and rove,
Hurled all ablaze up terraced grove,
And sparks, and snow, and smoke, and sleet
In angry circles waltzing meet,

33 No tent can stand, no blanket save
From biting blasts that round us rave;
With sleepless eyes, compelled to turn,—
One side to freeze, the other burn,—
We sigh for prayers of friends afar,
And long for laggard morning-star.

The storm is past, and azure skies
The orb of morn greet at its rise;
Soon warming rays dispel the gloom
That o'er our senses hung like doom,
And joyous hopes and buoyant tread
Gild halos bright o'er horrors fled.

Meanwhile, at dawn, on sullen shore,
With gravel filled and frozen o'er,
Our bark we found thus saved from wreck,
Keel-crushed, but firm her sides and deck;
And quick, with tools and comrades true,
In surf the frozen cobbles threw.

Her hold we bailed with battered pail,
Her keel repaired, unfurled her sail;
Our light stores shipped and rifles true,
Our rations short, and daring crew:
And, thankful for such lovely day,
With gentle breeze sailed up the bay.

But time were short to here relate
Our voyage o'er finger, thumb, or strait;
Round charming isle, o'er mystic hand,
To Indian cove, and thankful land,—
Then once again our steeds bestride,
And proudly o'er the meadows ride.

And here by lonely rill I find—
Sad trace of race to pale-face kind,
But feeble, few, and shy of men—
A wick-e-up of brush in glen,
And (blanket-robed for want of grave),
Last of his band, "Sheep-Eater" brave.

And now I pause and sadly think
Of cruel scenes ne'er traced in ink;
Of kindly words and acts of those
We curse and treat as savage foes,
[34] Yet practice crimes that dark disgrace
Our Christian creed and bearded race.

Thus pensive, wandering o'er the strand,
[35] Vases and urns from nature's hand,
Saucers and cups from hidden graves,
I see come rolling with the waves,
And marvel how a cause unknown
Could fashion neat such forms of stone!

Again, I view along the shore
Hot rills from hissing geysers pour,
[36] And finny forms beneath the wave
For angler's bait hot current brave,
To find, alas! like human fool,
A barb concealed and seething pool.

Again, a rill from melting snows
Adown thy turfy terrace flows,
To foam in sulphur pool as hot
As Sodom's slime in days of Lot!
[37] And thence from nauseous hissing rill
Sweet flow'ry vale with poisons fill.

[38] And islands thine, rock-ribbed and high,
With snowy crests amid the sky:
Inverted, mirrored 'neath the waves,
Seem isles to greet 'mid islands' graves;
And sylvan forms in fossil groves,
With vanished friends renew their loves.

Amid the mists of years to come,
With bunting, viol, harp, and drum,
Shall steamer proudly on her way,
Or safely moored in cove or bay,
Bear artist, poet, priest, and seer,
And ladies, ever smiling near.

And will they know or care for those
Who coasted capes through mists and snows?
Or pressed proud mountain-peaks to scale,
In summer storms or winter's gale?
And unknown islands wisely chose
As safe retreat from savage foes?

And oft, perchance, on island here,
With panther's tread pursued the deer
Or big-horn on the crests of snow,
Or grizzlies in the glens below,—
[39] For food their flesh, for hunting-shirt,
Their vacant coat with belt begirt?

And will they dream that garb so wild
Screened men of worth, refined and mild?
With sense to feel, with souls to love,
A lion's courage, hearts of dove,
Whose plans of life, if understood,
Were "suffer self for others' good"?

My voyage is o'er, its duties done,
This crystal shore my praise has won;
In other lands be mine to meet
Such golden sands and islands sweet,
And free from pelting storms of snow,
Ne'er scorching pits of sulphur know!
A long farewell,—I leave thy strand,—
Oh, "Mystic Lake" of "Wonder-Land!"

THE FAITHFUL LOVERS.

IN a smiling eastern valley, where the zephyrs dance and
 dally,
   Dwelt a maiden fair and blooming, and a yeoman tall
    and bold ;
Tender were the tears of parting of these lovers at his
    starting
   O'er the prairies and the coteaus, in his pilgrimage for
    gold.

For she dwells in halls.of splendor, where the heirs of
    wealth attend her,
   And her mother, sire, and brother seek with them
    alliance grand ;
But her plighted troth is given, pure, and registered in
    heaven,
   That her lover, heir of labor, she'll await from golden
    land.

"Love," he lisps, with eyelids quivering, "cease, oh,
    cease thy fears and grieving ;
   Hope will sweeten toil and danger of thy lover far
    away ;
Who, with glittering gems the rarest, and of mountain
    flowers the fairest,
   Bright will render this thy chamber, as for him thou
    kneel'st to pray."

In a vale of crystal fountains, deep amid the snowy
    mountains,
  Dwelt this toiler of the placer and this trailer of the
    deer;
And, although the painted savage ever lurked to slay and
    ravage,
  Still this ranger braved the danger with a soul that
    scoffed at fear.

For the mountain zephyrs laden whisper cheering words
    of maiden:
  "In my bosom ever loving dwell thy gems, and in my
    hair
Cluster wreaths of brilliant flowers, gathered in thy
    mountain bowers,
  And at even soars to heaven, for thy safety, fervent
    prayer."

Yet the wintry storms are dreary, and the trusting heart
    grows weary,
  When in waning moons no tidings thrill that loving
    breast so pure;
And within her home of splendor pride and fashion still
    attend her,
  And a courtly suitor wealthy seeks that love-lorn heart
    to cure.

Then from far-off lands came tidings of terrific war and
    fightings,
  By the fountains of the mountains, where the daring
    miners dwell;
Doleful dark-line pages filling scenes of death and valor
    thrilling,
  And a yeoman, slaughtering foeman, last and noblest
    of them, fell.

THE FAITHFUL LOVERS.

Not in words untimely spoken, but with loving heart-
    strings broken,
  Pales the maiden's cheeks so blooming, and in ago-
    nizing moan,
Heeding not the guests of splendor, nor her friends'
    consolings tender,
  Faintly throbbing, sinking sobbing, bursts her cry,
    "Alone! alone!"

Days are come and nights are banished, moons have
    waxed, and waned, and vanished,
  When a spectre from that chamber, pale and trembling,
    thin and wan,
On the arm of loving mother, and beside a tender brother,
  Slow, but eager, seeks the parlor, all to greet her lover
    gone.

"Comes he not?" she sighs in anguish; "for his greet-
    ing clasp I languish."
  "Oh, my Charlie, waits your Laurie, with the gems
    you sent afar.
Dwell you still beside the fountains, toiling 'mid the
    snowy mountains?
  Here I'll meet you, soon I'll greet you, or I'll wander
    where you are."

Lost were all their arts of cheering, kindly words and
    acts endearing;
  Only lover, daring rover, would her wandering dreams
    reveal;
All his bold, unselfish daring, all its fruits with Laurie
    sharing,
  And her cheering his appearing, could her clouded
    senses feel.

THE FAITHFUL LOVERS.

Fades the fever, slowly burning, tinged the cheek with health returning,
  And her vision, conquering reason, on its throne is crowned again;
When the vesper chimes are pealing, faintly through the twilight stealing,
  Came the story and the glory of her daring lover slain.

Slowly rallying, health regaining, soon, alas! with hectic waning,
  Prove the riven dart was driven to its feather in her soul;
And the flickering hope remaining of its earthly hope retaining
  Was a journey to some valley where the western billows roll.

Needless tale of preparation, nameless vale of destination,
  Faithful brother, would-be lover, press their wealth and tenderest care;
Zephyrs from the prairie blooming, lake of brine or mountain-looming,
  Hope sustaining, health regaining, till they reach a valley fair.

By a rill at eve reclining, 'neath the blooming roses twining,
  Lowly kneeling, love appealing, comes the youth, the brother's friend.
"Hist!" she cries, "these stars in heaven witnessed my betrothal given;
  Only Charlie will I marry, till life's pilgrimage shall end."

Vain his tears, his prayers and sighing; few, but firm,
   her words replying:
  "While on earth, or yet in heaven, his alone my life
     remains."
Rifles ringing, bullets singing, sudden death and terror
   bringing;
  Lover falling—sight appalling!—spouting gore her
     beauty stains.

Shrill the war-whoop thrills the valley; sharp the escort's
   answering rally;
  Steeds are dashing, sabres flashing, friends and foes
     commingled fall;
Lasso whirling, cruel slaying, blood-streams o'er the roses
   playing,—
  Daring brother, wounded lover, cheer the remnants,
     few and small.

Hand to hand they thrust and parry, and the fainting
   maiden carry
  To adobe hovel lowly; but the foe is there before.
Soon the swinging hatchet reeking, gleaming knife the
   trophies seeking,
  Demon yelling, scalp-lock swelling, witness grim the
     fight is o'er.

Hark! as swoop of eagles screaming, dashing steeds and
   sabres gleaming,
  "Rally! rally!" shouts in valley, down the savage ride
     and thrust;
First a plumed and stalwart ranger, charging grandly,
   scorning danger,
  Warriors meeting, chieftain seeking, plume and bonnet
     kiss the dust.

THE FAITHFUL LOVERS.

Savage, ere his safety seeking, carves from slain the
    trophy reeking;
Gory chieftain, clasping maiden,—"Mine," he cries,
    "this golden hair!"
Hatchet arm by blade is riven, and in breast to hilt is
    driven,
By the stranger belted ranger, whose arm sustains the
    sinking fair.

Heeds he not the dying rattle, savage chief, or shout of
    battle,
Only seeing maiden clinging to his breast for refuge
    given.
Beaming eyes again are meeting, loving lips again are
    greeting,—
"Oh, my Charlie!"—"Darling Laurie!"—met on
    earth instead of heaven.

Oh, that stalwart brave is quivering, and in Laurie's arms
    is sinking,
For an arrow to its feather, vile, has pierced that
    manly form.
"Laurie, love, we've met and parted," faint he whispers;
    broken-hearted,
Courage-nerving, maiden loving stanches crimson
    spouting warm.

Painted brave, from hidden cover, leaps to slay the sink-
    ing lover;
All in horror, as the warrior comes, with bright and
    deadly blade,

In her robes of maiden, loving, glares she as a warrior daring;
On he dashes—pistol flashes—chieftain at her feet is laid!

THE DARING MAIDEN.

Quick she rends the shirt of leather, quick withdraws the cruel feather,—
"Tis your Laurie, oh, my Charlie!"—on his lips her kisses pours;
Then with silken bandage holy, through the rents of buckskin lowly,
Checks the ebbing tide of crimson, and the sinking life restores.

When the bloody fray was over, and the dead they needs
 must cover,
 Found the brother dead, but lover, scalped and gory,
  lingering still:
"Die I cannot ere confessing crime my guilty soul dis-
 tressing,—
 Listen, Charlie! pardon, Laurie!" thus his moaning
  accents thrill.

"Laurie, when I watched thy chamber, missive came
 from mountain ranger;
 I, in envy, love, and frenzy, took and bore it to my
  room;
Well I knew the manly writing proof he lived, and hence
 the blighting
 Of my planning, guile, and cunning, and defeat my
  certain doom.

"Villain! then I read the story of his daring deeds and
 glory:
 How the savage slay and ravage, how from gaping
  wounds he fell;
But amidst the yells appalling he escaped by crafty crawl-
 ing;
 Hence these thrilling pages filling to the maiden loved
  so well.

"Then with love and envy swelling, perjured soul to
 Satan selling,
 I as brother kind and tender told in strains of fondest
  love
Tale of sickness short and trying, Laurie's love, and
 peaceful dying,
 And to lover message tender that in bliss they'd meet
  above.

"From that hour I writhed in torture, with grinning fiends will be my future,
  Unforgiven, cursed of heaven!" words his last amidst his groans;
Startled lovers, backward scanning, see the web of demons planning,
  And, forgiving, leave the erring with the God who sin atones.

Days have come and weeks are ended, moons have waned and years have blended;
  In a valley pilgrims dally, 'mid the field of love and gore,
On a marble shaft ascending names of fallen ones are blending;
  Fading echoes from the vespers thrill the tendrils twining o'er.

And a stately mansion looming, in that vale of roses blooming,
  Chariots mowing, vintage flowing, o'er uncounted leagues of land,
While a matron bland and comèly, and a statesman grand and courtly,
  With their children tall and blooming, greet their guests with welcome grand.

Painting, bright as wealth can render, portray in that hall of splendor
  Belted yeoman facing foeman, hatchet raised in deadly strife;
Tall and lovely maiden clinging, 'neath a reeking hatchet swinging
  O'er her brother, to her lover Heaven's vengeance guides his knife!

And upon the lofty ceiling, painted with historic feeling,
    Gory chieftain, lovely maiden, wounded ranger faint between
Chief, from pistol-muzzle reeling, maiden o'er her lover kneeling,
    Crimson stanching, without blanching, real as in life are seen.

GALLANT CHARLEY REYNOLDS.

[40] Once the chosen scout of Stanley,
    Often Ludlow's mountain guide,
Then with me erst true and manly,—
    Thou who with our Custer died!
Over all the Big-horn Mountains,
    And beside the coteau's cone,
'Mid Missouri's geyser fountains,
    And along the Yellowstone.

Kind and cheerful was thy bearing,
    Firm and martial was thy tread;
First amongst the brave and daring
    Art thou numbered with the dead.
Bravely thou, with Reno valiant,
    And with crafty Bloody-Knife,
In the front of charge most gallant,
    O'er the ford of bloody strife.

Fearless when thy steed was falling,
    Hatchet hewn, and pierced by lance;
'Mid the flood and foe appalling,
    Demon-like was thy advance!
Pistol puff and ring of rifle,
    Flashing knife and hatchet gleam;
Reeking scalp and sinking stifle,
    Dying yell in dashing stream!

Ghastly strewing fast around thee
  Painted braves and plumes of those
Thy carbine slaughtered, still surround thee
  Circling hordes of yelling foes.
All in vain were deeds of daring,
  All too swift and sad thy doom!
Earth's last view was savage glaring,—
  The encrimsoned stream thy tomb!

Stricken in thy youth and beauty,
  Sadly stricken ere thy prime;
Fallen at the ford of duty,
  Lo! an honored name is thine!
Charley! may the foe who slew thee
  Ever bear a tainted name!
Reynolds! all the friends who knew thee
  Shall award thee lofty fame!

Peaceful home has me delivered
  From the fate that war attends;
Desert flowers have bloomed and withered
  O'er the bones of mountain friends·
Sternly fate—not of our choosing—
  Severs us forever here;
Sadly thus, with memory musing,
  Darkly fades the fated year!

Other friends along that river
  Fought and fell to rise no more,
Yielding their souls to God, the Giver,
  When the deadly strife was o'er;

When along the Yellowstone
   Peace and happiness shall reign
O'er gory fields both lost and won,
   None shall say they died in vain.

Can daring deeds of human hand
   Save the soul beyond the grave?
And are there in that spirit-land
   Mansions for the true and brave?
Oh, God of justice, but of love,
   Judge them by their deeds and light!
And in thy blissful home above
   Grant them garlands at thy right!

"PILGRIMS OF THE YELLOWSTONE.

A BAND of modern pilgrims went prospecting for gold,
And rode or drove their horses as in the days of old;
The Mississippi and Missouri obstruct their path in vain,
And they pioneer'd the railway in roving o'er the plain.

The Platte they left at Laramie, with visions bright of mines
Amid the Big-horn Mountains or gulches dark with pines,
And placers in the cañons, or charming hills and dales,
For peaceful homes of plenty amid the fertile vales.

Then 'long the beauteous coteau, rolling like the waves,
'Mid bison, elk, and antelope, and, often, Indian braves;
The *first* they chased to slaughter, the *latter* chased to slay:
Sometimes they were pursuers, but oft pursued were they.

Through ever-changing fortune, with caution, dash, and arms,
They passed the Cactus Desert and the Indian's fierce alarms;
Then mountain above terrace beside their trail arose,—
In the last a rocky cañon, on the first eternal snows.

Fountains, bright sunny fountains, dispel their thirsty fears;
Mountains, oh, snowy mountains, loud they greet with cheers!

Time, toil, and patience conquer, and from the frozen
   crest,
Deep 'mid the lava mountains, they view a park of rest.

Cedar-bordered rivulets descended from the snow,
Roamed countless on the pampas the shaggy buffalo;
O'er all, in autumn's beauty, the mellow sunbeams
   shone,—
A matchless vale of verdure along the Yellowstone!

With game-trout teemed the waters, all bounteous the
   soil,
Gold-dust in the placers, awaiting only toil
Of famished eastern labor, the thrifty and the bold,
To rear their rugged cabins and garner up the gold.

Eager adown the mountain, lured by the brilliant sheen
Of gushing valley-fountain, begirt with emerald green:
"Oh, here's the happy valley, this is the lovely West;
Here we no longer dally, but build us homes of rest!"

But since Adam sinned in Eden, and Eve to hide their
   shame
Of fig-leaves made them aprons, earth has ever been the
   same:
The vales of blooming roses are beset with piercing
   thorns,
And death is ever garnering what beauty most adorns.

Thus to our weary pilgrims peaceful the valley seems:
Glowing are their camp-fires, sweet their golden dreams;
When shrill the war-whoop echoes! sharp the rifle rings!
Cruel pierce the arrows, high the hatchet swings!

Vainly rouse the startled sleepers! swift a circling gleam
Of scalping-knife descending, and then the dying scream!
Quick wrenched is reeking trophy,—soon amid the gloom
Coyote fierce and famished grant the gory dead a tomb.

From that sickening scene of horror one alone e'er reached his home,
Thence from rural peace and comfort naught again can bid him roam;
'Mid tales of gold in Black Hills or along the Rosebud vale
Ghosts arise of friends in "Bad Lands," and of gore along the trail.

Mothers dear and sweethearts loving awaited their return in vain;
Drear the homes and sad the kindred they'll revisit ne'er again;
Long and vain for absent loved ones were their kindred's sighs and moans,—
Painted braves and dusky maidens alike deride their bleaching bones.

But the fearful fate of Custer on the fated Little Horn
All too late aroused our people to uproot the Rosebud thorn;*
In the coming tramps and battles fallen friends shall we bemoan,
But no peace shall greet the Sioux ere they leave the Yellowstone.

---

* "Rosebud thorn," Sitting Bull. A Rosebud, or Un-ca-pap-pa, Sioux chief.

Then beside the desert coteau and the crimson Little Horn,
As along the Mystic River of the spouting geyser born,
Miners wealth in peace shall gather from the placer's golden sand,
Pilgrims health in joy shall garner in the lofty "Wonder-Land."

CAPTIVE MAIDEN.

"Rise, my muse, sing of a maiden
    Captive on the coteau wild;
Not with golden ringlets laden,
    But tresses raven, Nature's child.

From the camp of slaughtered Cheyenne,
    Near the crimson Custer plain,
Rode she to the border stockade,
    Weeping in the captive train.

Long she looked and sighed for lover,
    Chieftain of a mountain band,
First in fight, and last to hover
    On trail of foe in native land.

But her longing eyes grew weary,
    And her loving heart grew faint,
In a prison, chill and dreary,
    Child of freedom in restraint.

When her kindred yield to capture,
    Weary of the scourge of war,
Glows her cheek and form with rapture
    At chieftain's totem from afar.

Proud he stood amid the warriors,
   In the glare of council fire;
"First," quoth he, "release my maiden,
   Or you shall feel my ire.

"I, of mountain clan the chieftain,
   I in freedom chose a mate:
Only free she'll wed War-Eagle,
   Be it life or death, my fate."

"Trail your totem, yield your pinto,
   Quick disarm your warriors all;
"Mine be teepee," says the pale-face,
"And upon our mercy call."

"This," quoth the chief, "to me, a warrior?
   I disarm?—be squaw and slave?—
Teepee for friend, for foeman hatchet,—
   From his war-horse dies the brave."

War-whoop shrill, and mounted warriors,
   Lance and plume, bedeck the plain;
Fierce the onset, long the struggle,
   The maid to save,—alas! in vain.

Saw the morning carnage ghastly,—
   Gory harvest on the plain;
Blanket-strewed and bullet-furrowed,
   Desert moistened, not by rain.

Gone the chieftain, gone the remnant
   Of his warriors, faint and few;
In court of prison slept the maiden,—
   Moist her tresses, not with dew.

Vain had been her pray'r for freedom;
　Guard and bay'net barr'd the door:
" This will open gate to prison,—
　Moulder clay and spirit soar."

Thus she speaks; then, tall and stately,
　Bares her bosom, looks above:
" God of red-man,—oh, Man-i-tou!
　Thus I come, a bride of love."

Quick as swoop of mountain-eagle
　Heart is pierced by blade in hand;
Marks the rill of gushing crimson,
　Freedom's trail to Spirit-land.

THE WONDER-LAND.

Ho, ye pilgrims, seeking pleasure,
  Or for health in vain,
Listen to me, while I truly
  Tell where both to gain.

Chorus.

'Mid encircling snowy mountains,
  Falls and cañons grand,
Bathing-pools and spouting fountains,
  Of the "Wonder-Land."

There, enraptured, have I wandered
  Through the glades and dells,
Where the big-horn, elk, and beaver
  Each in freedom dwells.

Where the azure pools of healing
  Terrace from the snow,
Like a glist'ning cascade frozen,
  To the glens below.

Where the spray from spouting fountains
  Forms a halo crest,
Looming up the snowy mountains
  Rainbows where they rest.

Where the halo's quivering shadows,
    O'er the Triple Falls,
Tint the cañon, where wild waters
    Echo 'long its walls.

Where the swan with snowy plumage,
    Brant, and crested drake,
O'er the yellow trout and speckled,
    Skim the crystal lake.

Where the screams of mountain-lion
    Pierce the midnight air,
Like the fabled Indian warrior
    Wailing in despair.

Where the moose and curly bison,
    Monarchs of the glades,
Like the mammoth loom in roaming
    'Mid the twilight shade.

Where the ancient forests vernal,
    Now in lava cased,
Matchless opal, crystal caskets,
    Ruthless are defaced.

Where thin-crusted earth seems bending
    From the fires below,
Threat'ning, as of old, the rending
    And lava overflow.

Where the bowers of Eden, blooming
    'Mid the glens of earth,
Nestle, 'neath fierce tempests howling,
    Like creation's birth.

Where on earth are matchless blended
Vernal flowers and snow,
Eden glens and glens of sulphur,
Elysium and woe.

43 Oh, for wisdom in the councils
Of our nation great,
To protect these matchless wonders
From a ruthless fate!

BOLD HERO OF THE BORDER.

(GEN. NELSON D. MILES.)

Born in the land of Pilgrims, beside its granite shore,
Thy lullaby of freedom the waves unfettered roar,
And, rearing as a yeoman, amid its Northern vales,
Thy heart defends thy country when Southern foe assails;
And youthful form waxed stalwart thy trusty sword to wield,
In craggy pass of mountain or crimson sulphur field,
Till loyal hosts in triumph forced treason's clans to yield.

On furlough brief from battle, thy eager soul did burn
To abler serve thy country and worthy laurels earn;
Then o'er the distant prairies and sterile thorny plains,
Amid the rolling coteau the Mystic River drains,
The wild terrific gulches and snowy mountain-crest,
The war-trail of the savage thy daring footsteps pressed,
Bold hero of the border, by all its people blest.

The bold Nez-Perce chieftain, from valley of the West,
Descending to the coteau from snowy mountain-crest,
Safe crossed the Mystic River, and then Missouri's wave,
The matchless mountain trailer, bold leader of the brave,
"In lair of hidden gulches, in Woody Mountain wilds,
On Crow and Ree and Sturgis in proud derision smiles,
Yet found on trail to Britain just one too many "Miles."

For then by matchless marching o'er desert pass and plain,
And floods of mighty rivers which snowy mountains drain,

Like phalanx of the Grecian, thou led'st thy vet'ran band,
Where conflicts are decided in struggle hand to hand;
For there with sword and hatchet in gulch with no retreat,
Each with a worthy foeman who never knew defeat,
The Che-nook and the Eagle in final conflict meet.

Each with a prayer for loved ones; the latter's far away,—
The first's in coula hidden, in trembling terror lay,
'Mid deadly ring of rifle and scorching sulphur smoke;
The reeking lance and hatchet and sword's descending stroke,
The chieftain's battle-rally and answering Eagle's scream,
Commingled coat and blanket in gushing crimson stream,
Till bright through storm and carnage white Che-nook flag is seen.

⁴⁵ Then came the parley herald,—no servile cringing foe,
But chieftain with his rifle, the victors' terms to know,
To save his wife and children and remnant of his band,—
"Surrender!" says the Eagle; "these warriors understand
The mercy, truth, and honor I tender fallen foe,
Oft taking to my service the warriors that I know!"
And thus the tide of crimson in mercy ceased to flow.

And now, bold border chieftain, pray listen to a friend,
With matchless nerve and daring may thoughts of loved ones blend?
Thy prudence, skill, and courage are themes of praise by all,
And needed still by country. Beside, wert thou to fall,
No laurel wreath of vict'ry could cheer thy lonely home,
Hush widow's wails, or orphans', in this cold world alone;
More cautious prove, O chieftain! when duty calls to roam.

STALWART YEOMAN.

⁴⁶ Not from hall of the Washburns,
    Who so long have honor'd Maine,
But lowly "Buckeye" cabin
    Our stalwart yeoman came.
Not from classic Oberlin,
    Ever in freedom's van,—
Self-taught, with chain and compass,
    Wild border-lines he ran,
And from nature's God in wildwood
    Well learned the rights of man.

Oh, well do I remember
    The days when we were young,
On our shoulders trusty rifles,
    And from belts sharp hatchets hung.
Such training made us soldiers
    In freedom's darkest hour;
And the confidence of comrades,
    When the bloody strife was o'er,
Gave him the seat in Congress
    Of Dan Voorhees—"Sycamore."

From the halls of legislation,*
    When our duty there was done,
We met amid the mountains,
    Far towards the setting sun.

---

* His duties were thus in the councils of the nation, mine in the less prominent position of a member of the Legislature of Ohio.

I trailed down the Columbia,
   He traced up the Yellowstone
To the geysers of Wyoming
   And lava cañon lone,
Where halos lure but poison,
   And turned his footsteps home
To distant Wabash valley,
   Thence never more to roam.

Cold rest the clods of Wabash,
   Piled on his patriot breast;
Chill howl the storms of winter
   Round Mount Washburn's rocky crest.
Warm glowed his form with ardor
   When freedom's flag he bore;
Warm thrilled his heart for loved one
   'Mid the desert tempests' roar.
Tender their tears of greeting
   When the toils of life were o'er;
Sweet 'mid the bowers of Eden
   May they dwell for evermore.

GO WHERE DUTY CALLS THEE.

Go where duty calls thee,
Or where hope enthralls thee,
   O'er mountain, lake, or glade;
Where the wild man roameth,
Or the wild wind moaneth,
   Deep 'mid the forest shade;
Where the turtle cooing,
Or the bison lowing,
'Neath the wild storm brewing,
   Would I be dear to thee?
In a cavern screening
Thee from tempest screaming,
   Wilt thou remember me?

When by spouting fountains,
'Mid the snowy mountains,
   In the Park of Mystery,
From thy couch of flowers,
In enchanting bowers,
   Oft wilt thou sigh for me?
And from halos pouring
O'er wild waters roaring,
Like proud eagle soaring,
   Oh, will thy spirit free,
O'er white mountains looming,
Or bright prairies blooming,
   Often revisit me?

When fierce foes a legion,
In some lowly region,
  Beleague thy mountain camp,
And, from watching dreary,
This lovèd form grows weary,
  Cold its turfy couch and damp,
In thy fitful dreaming
Will these bright eyes beaming,
Or in sorrow streaming,
  Like angels visit thee?
All in anguish quaking,
From thy vision waking,
  Oh, wilt thou welcome me?

When from leaden rattle
Of terrific battle
  Smoke hides the light of day,
And from hatchet gleaming
Crimson tide is streaming
  In visions far away,
From the gory lying,
Hear the moans and sighing
  Of bosom dear to thee,
Lisp will latest whisper
Dearer name than sister,
  And sacred all to me?

THE DYING MANDANS.

Beneath the rolling coteau,
    Beside the roaring flood,
Dwelt the race of the Man-i-tou,
    Mandans of the better blood.

Their earth-lodge homes of plenty,
    From tillage of the soil,
Enticed the Sioux robbers
    To plunder and despoil.

Slaughtered amid the gardens,
    And driven from the plain,
Smallpox among the wardens,
    Missouri's bath was vain.

Death's last relentless gleaner
    Swept maidens young and fair;
Warriors with plume and streamer
    Lay dying everywhere.

Where, then, were Clarke and Catlin?
    Where Irving, Camp, and Stone?
With Brule and smallpox battling,
    They sank and died alone!

[47] Oh, ghastly scene of horror!
   Oh, ghastly town of doom!
No hope in dawn of morrow,
   No halo 'mid the gloom.

Thus sank the Ree and Mandan,
   No friends to cheer or save;
Thus dying in abandon,
   And for the dead no grave.

Long years have come and vanished,
   Crumbling each earth-lodge home;
Long have the remnant banished
   Ceased o'er the site to roam.

By Little Horn's green valley—
   Beyond the Yellowstone—
Sioux, Brule, and Teton rally,
   The pale-face dead have strewn.

Long years again shall vanish,
   And Custer, Cook, and Blue,—
Their honors none would banish
   From lists of heroes true.

And Reynolds,—noble Charley,—
   And Mandan,—Bloody-Knife,—
Who ever scorned to parley,
   But fighting gave their life!

THE DYING TRAPPER.

PEERLESS the park of fountains!
  Far, oh, far below
Its circling crests of mountains,
  Begirt with ice and snow!

⁴⁸ Hard by those spouting fountains,
  Far, oh, far away!
Done with his frays and scoutings,
  A dying trapper lay:

One reared in wealth and kindness,—
  Sad, oh, sad the day!
When blighted love and blindness
  Allured his feet astray.

Long years have come and vanished,—
  Time, oh, time has flown!
Since rudely scorned and banished
  To tread the wilds alone.

But on that gloomy morning
  Screams, oh, screams, and yells,—
Of death and ravage warning,—
  Rang through the glades and dells!

Gory and scalped around him,
  Cold, oh, cold and dead!
Were cherished friends who bound him
  To home and vision fled.

THE DYING TRAPPER.

Remnant soon of comrades rally,—
  Few, oh, few, and sad!
"Boys," he says, "dark seems the valley,
  Oh, gently raise my head!

"Brothers, Life's crimson tide is flowing,—
  Soon, oh, soon 'twill cease!
Lone through cañon dark I'm going
  To gulch of Woe or glen of Peace.

"Comrades, long we've roamed together!
  Drear, oh, drear, we part!
Deadly storms scowl o'er the heather,—
  Dim's the trail to Heaven's Park.

"But portrait from my bosom never
  Death, oh, death, shall part!
Piercing arrow does not sever,
  But pinions Laura to my heart!

"By thy beck'ning hand invited,
  Love, oh, love, I come!
Severed in life,—in death united,
  We'll evermore be one!"

BOZEMAN BOLD.

A TALE of guide, who daring band
From Platte led safe through desert sand,
Wild Big-horn gulch and cañon lone,
To mountain gate of Yellowstone;
No bridge, no boat, no friend to hail,
And painted warriors on their trail.

Mild autumn days are waning fast,
Round mountain-peak howls wintry blast;
For sheltered vale of Gallatin
Pilgrim and guide are dashing in,—
Bull-boat and raft, mustang and mule,
At war-path ford of Crow and Brule.

In rival bands last crest they scale
By Bozeman's Pass and Bridger's Trail;
"White men and tents,"—oh, glorious sheen
Of murm'ring rill and pastures green!
A town they plant, but wait for fame
Of daring deed to christen name.

Too soon, alas! for ranger brave,
Pilgrim beleaguered, on trail to save,
In vision bright, on coteau wild,
Saw sainted wife and darling child.
"Husband and sire, no longer roam;
In morn thou'lt soar to us and home."

By camp-fire dim on Yellowstone
Spake daring guide to comrade lone:
"Up, comrade, up! grasp rifle soon!
Swift pinto mount, and dash from doom!
Leave me to fate, my toils are o'er;
Soon friends I'll greet on brighter shore."

As comrade halts, kind words to say,
"Quick, saddle horse, and haste away!"
He cries; when lo! adown the glen,
On loping steeds dash painted men.
With rifle poised he ready stands
Till spouting gore stains desert sands.

Comrade escaped,—sad tale to tell,—
Returning, found him as he fell.
Rifle and scalp, pistol and plume,
Sure, phantom-warriors caused the doom
Chèyenne and Crow oft tried in vain,
And pass and town bear Bozeman's name.

THE CLOUD-CIRCLED MOUNTAINS.

[52] My heart's in the mountains, my heart's not at home;
Though here cluster blessings, I still love to roam.
My heart's with my pinto, my rifle and belt,
Where big-horn and beaver forever have dwelt.
Oh, my heart's 'mid the fountains and streamlets below
The cloud-circled mountains, white-crested with snow!

My heart's 'mid the mirage, the lakes, and the plains,
The buttes and the coteaus, where wild nature reigns;
My heart's 'mid the coulees and cañons so grand,
And bright-spouting geysers of lone Wonder-Land.
Oh, my heart's 'mid those fountains and streamlets below
Those cloud-circled mountains, white-crested with snow!

My heart's by the camp-fires of trappers so bold,
The tents and the teepees of warriors of old;
My heart's down the river, whose torrents loud roar
In greeting the billows on surf-beaten shore.
Oh, my heart's 'mid the fountains, whence trout streamlets flow
'Mid cloud-circled mountains, white-crested with snow!

My heart's in the valleys and parks of the West,
'Mid deer, elk, and grizzly, of all game the best.
Farewell to my business, farewell to my home;
Adieu to my loved ones, my fate is to roam
'Mid the pure crystal fountains and geysers below
The wild-circling mountains, white-glistening with snow.

My heart's 'mid old forests by lava o'erthrown,
Now crystals of opal and amethyst-stone,
Chalcedony casket (for Manitou's heart),
And brilliant enamel unrivalled by art.
Oh, my heart's 'mid such caverns 'neath the lava o'erflow
From once fiery mountains, now buried in snow!

My heart glows with ardor to gather and learn
New lessons of science, if spared to return;
If mine be to perish, may Heaven bestow
A tomb in lone grotto deep hidden in snow!
Oh, my heart's 'mid the fountains and grottos below
The cloud-circled mountains, white-crested with snow!

WHERE ELSE ON EARTH?

⁵³ Where else on earth does water furnish
    Rocky evidence so strong
Of its power to build and burnish,
    As this terrace, high and long?

Chorus.

Where the peerless pools for healing
    From their ruins 'mid the snow,
Each, with waters health restoring,
    Terrace to the glens below.

Dim, amid the ages vanished,
    Snowy waters laughing poured,
Through the valley, and in cañon,
    Loud, in falls and rapids, roared.

Then from womb of fires smothered
    Broad were yawning fissures rent,
And o'er mists from seething waters
    Rainbows ever beauteous blent.

'Twas a new creation forming,
    Geysers, matchless at their birth;
Round their hissing funnels building
    Marble forms unknown to earth.

In the ages slowly passing,
   From these rents of hidden fire
Spouts the min'ral-laden waters,
   Terrace ever building higher.

Till athwart the cañon yawning,
   Firm a rocky barrier rose,—
With the severed waters forming
   Mountain-lake amid the snows.

54 Long its waves, by tempest driven,
   Fiercely lashed its seething shore;
Fire and flood in conflict fearful
   'Mid the clouds terrific roar.

But the power ever waning
   Of the smothered fire of woe
Left the crests with forests circled,
   And new funnels formed below.

55 Then the ever-lashing billows
   Rent a gap in mountain-side,
And the wild escaping waters
   Carved a cañon deep and wide.

Still the all-eroding waters
   Undermined the crests of snow,
Hurling funnel, tree, and terrace,
   Crushed and mingled, far below.

56 Hence these ruins weird and fearful,
   And the cliffs so white and grand,
And these crumbling cones of geysers,
   Still the pride of Wonder-Land.

BRADLEY THE BRAVE.

[57] Last of a race of warriors who served their country well,
In glen of distant mountains foremost thou fighting fell;
The promise of a hero, in thy maiden-march through rain
In the mountains of Virginia, has proven not in vain.
E'en now as then I view thee expand from boy to man,
When the opening roar of battle first found thee in the van,
Ever thy choice of duty where crimson torrents ran.

When strength of sire was sinking from suffering in the field
Thy youthful arm waxed stalwart the battle-blade to wield;
In every post of duty, of danger, or of skill,
Matchless was thy endurance, thy iron nerve and will;
Until the flag of freedom, of union, and of love,
O'er fiery clans of treason in triumph soared above
With the pinion of the eagle and the plumage of the dove.

Then hastening to the border, thou eager sought to know
The hidden haunts of Blackfoot, of Sioux, and of Crow;
And boldly, with thy vet'rans, in craggy pass or plain,
Or valleys of the rivers the snowy mountains drain,
Thou fearless trailed the savage, the innocent to save,—

Though summer's sun is scorching or winter's tempest
    rave,—
On all the border honored, bold leader of the brave.

But halo days are ended, and sorrow is come,
With the stalwart Nez-Perces from setting of sun,
In the vanguard of Gibbon, first flash lays thee low,
Still thy battle-blade clasping, firm facing the foe;
'Mid the heaps of slain comrades tho'rt deluged in gore,
Cold and stern is thy visage,—thy conflicts are o'er,
And the war-whoop of savage shall rouse thee no more!

Far away art thou sleeping in silence and peace,
Friends and kindred are weeping,—in joy let them cease;
Thy sore-stricken parents rejoice in a son,
A hero, whose laurels were gallantly won;
Thy State and thy country in gratitude save
From sorrow thy loved ones, and green o'er thy grave
Twine the myrtle and laurel, O Bradley the brave!

FROM BIG-HORN'S BLEAK MOUNTAINS.

⁵⁹ From Big-horn's bleak mountains white glistening with
  snow,
The Big-horn's bright fountains through green meadows
  flow,
Or, skipping and dashing in rapids or falls,
In fury loud lashing their deep cañon walls;
Then 'mid the long coteaus by roses o'ergrown
Rush its floods to their greeting the bold Yellowstone.

In all these green valleys from river to snow,
Where autumn long dallies, are cairns of the Crow;
The harvest of battles with Rick-a-ree brave,
And Sioux or Blackfoot, their country to save;
Where warm are the winters and countless the game
Of bison and "big-horn,"—"wild sheep,"—hence the
  name.

But vain were all efforts with Sioux for peace;
Ne'er silent was war-whoop, ne'er signal-fires cease,
⁶⁰ Till Custer from Rosebud saw valley as sweet
As glens where the spirits of warriors shall meet,
And in his last rally, 'mid plumed crested braves,
Led phalanx of heroes to glory,—not graves!

Here Bridger and Bozeman, in crusade for gold,
Led pilgrims and miners and mountaineers bold;

Fierce fighting the Sioux—but kind was the Crow—
In passes of mountains or valleys below,—
" And Farrer and comrades passed safely along
Sweet valley, now famous for slaughter and song.

O'er all these long coteaus, from mountain to plain,
In all these broad valleys that mountain floods drain,
Each park 'mid the forests, and each glen 'mid the snow,
Are dwindling the warriors, are fading the Crow;
And soon shall the ploughshare of pale-face turn o'er
The sites of their teepees, once crimson with gore,—
The bones of a people who wander no more!

MYSTIC LAND.

"OH, tell me, I pray thee, my comrade and friend,
In Mystic Land only do wonders so blend?
Bright fountains, bleak mountains unrivalled in form,
Commingling, encircling, in sunshine and storm;
And geysers and salses eject from below
Hot water and sulphur from regions of woe,
With moanings and groanings, like wails of the lost,
From funnels of fire encircled by frost!

"There big-horn and bison calm graze in the glade,
Near grizzly and lion, low crouched in the shade;
Where throbbings and flowings of hot springs and streams
Build cascades of marble, reflecting in gleams;
Cliff-buttressed, tall turrets, white glistening in snow,
Are mirrored in lakelets unfathomed below;
And bendings and rendings of thin crust of earth,
In quivering convulsions, like travail of birth;
Hot water in chaldrons by cold lake and brook,
For boiling, still floundering, live trout on the hook.

"Where rubies bright sparkle in caskets of stone,
Of cedars and balsams by lava o'erflown;
And crystals in grottos e'er glisten and gleam
In visions unrivalled save Aladdin's dream;
Near caverns of sulphur as hissing and hot
As slime vales of Sodom in legend of Lot;

And mist-sheen and echo, from cascades and falls,
With beauty and music enliven their walls;
And coule and cañon, deep-furrowed by time,
Are terraced and tinted, unique and sublime ;
And rainbow and halo encircle the sheen
Of geysers reflected in lakelets of green !"

" Hist, comrade ! I claim there is not on this earth
Its rival in beauty, in wonders, or worth ;
For surely here nature has gathered to show
In marvels commingled all mortals should know ;
Of planet formation its growth and decay,
As childhood to manhood, and fading away ;
Where ramble and romance insure from despair
The victims of sickness, of sorrow, and care,
And science, in strata, new pages unfold
Of structure and crystal in forests of old ;
Lo ! Christians, in meekness, in faith, and in love,
Seek from wonders below their Creator above."

THE GRANGER SONG.

[62] Oh, my rural friend and neighbor,
    If inclined to roam,
Listen to me while I truly
    Say, Why stay at home.

Chorus.

Keep the farm, my rural neighbor,
    Hold the plough or drive;
Drain your swamps, read well, and labor,
    Frugal live and thrive.

In the passing years depressing
    Countless homes are sold
On a mortgage for a trifle,
    Lost in search of gold.

Some in cities seek professions
    Already overgrown;
Others business all unfitting,
    Now their *luck* bemoan.

Some the prairies and the valleys
    Of the boundless West,
Though alluring, found deceiving,
    And are sore distressed.

THE GRANGER SONG.

Oh, the hunger, toil, and danger
   Of the thirsty plain,
Or in gulches of the pilgrim,
   Seeking gold in vain!

Cold the clods and rude the coffin
   O'er some loving breast;
Thus unwisely, all untimely,
   Hasten'd to his rest.

Neither mountain, gem, nor valley
   Should entice to roam
From the blessings ever nestling
   'Round an eastern home.

Oh, ye lassies, early blooming,
   Harbor not the beau
Who is witty—more's the pity—
   From the wine's o'erflow.

And ye Grangers, seeking knowledge
   In our rural schools,
Wisely choose the yeoman college,—
   'Tis no place for fools.

Long and narrow seems the furrow
   As a road to wealth;
Yet pursuing is insuring
   Honor, home, and health.

Plant the chestnut, yew, and balsam,
   Ash and vernal pine,
Arbor-vitæ hedge 'round orchard,
   Peach and trellis'd vine.

Hold the homestead of your father;
    Leave it to your son ;
Leave it better than you found it
    When your work is done.

Build your school-rooms, rear your churches,
    And sustain them too ;
Be to temperance, truth, and virtue
    Ever just and true.

BORDER BRAVE.

(GENERAL N. D. MILES.)

Vict'ry again, thou border brave,
  Snatched from the jaws of fate;
Through flood or flame to battle save
  Thou never wert too late.

Nez-Perce's, chief of gallant race,
  Proud leader on the trail,
In Gibbon's charge and Howard's chase
  Proved fearful to assail.

Through glade and glen in Wonder-Land
  His stalwart warriors came,
Tourists to save 'mid geysers grand
  Plead innocence in vain.

When winding from the snowy crest,
  Or dashing o'er the plain,
The crafty Crow, and Sturgis pressed
  Upon his trail in vain.

Then o'er Missouri's turbid flood
  He all pursuers scorns,
Yet on the trail to Sitting Bull
  Found Woody Mountain thorns.

There, trailer thou on mountain-path,
   And victor of the dales,
As screaming eagle swoops in wrath,
   The fearful foe assails.

Thy vet'rans bold charge as of old,
   'Mid storm and leaden rain,
And daring scout and comrades bold
   Are numbered with the slain

[63] Not unavenged, for Looking-Glass
   And countless warriors brave
No more will ambush in the pass,
   But fill a warrior's grave.

The white flag floats for fight to cease;
   Then pleads the chief to save
The remnant of his band, and peace
   Of gallant Border Brave.

THE TATTOOED ARTIST.

"I SING of an artist, scribe, poet, and seer,
A lover of nature and scoffer at fear,
Who longed in his childhood, and yearned as a man,
For a steed on the border, a sword in the van,
And a couch on the field where the red torrents ran.

At school oft the figures would marshal as men,
Fierce braves on the coteau, or scouts in the glen;
His brush, as an artist, the lilies would scorn,
And glory in painting the cactus and thorn,
Or the crests of his warriors with plumes would adorn.

As a poet, o'erlooking the beauties of home,
His themes are of artists and warriors who roam,—
Tall, portly, and stalwart, with long, wavy hair,
A hero he seems in the eyes of the fair,
And his lyrics the patrons of science ensnare.

And thus he arranges a tourist to go
O'er the plains and the rivers and mountains of snow,
To note while he journeys, and write when at rest,
And paint the proud warriors and steeds of the West,
To publish in journals of science the best.

With outfit unrivalled, hope buoyant and strong,
He hies for the regions of slaughter and song;
All cheerful his parting with patrons and friends,
But tears fleck the tokens a fond mother sends,
And the cheeks of one dearer, whose locket attends.

Our hero a listener to lectures had been,
Which portray the white man as primitive sin;
While, lo! the poor Indian is ever in need,
Bereft of his birthright and robbed of his steed,
Safe prey for the pale-face, his lust, and his greed.

And Catlin he'd envied, and Cooper perused,
On their tales and their paintings in sympathy mused,
'Till love for his race as a people had fled;
No fear on the border save of those who had said,
"The only good Indians are those who are dead."

Thus blithe from the portals of science and lore,
He hies to the regions of ambush and gore;
On a craft of the rivers, released from restraint,
In tracings of nature, wild, brilliant, or quaint,
He revels with brushes, pen, pencil, and paint.

"Oh, ho!" says our artist, "quick land me again,"
As a village of teepees he spies on the plain;
"I'll show you the spirit of Catlin survives,
And fears not the warriors, dog-soldiers, or wives!"
"They're painters all, too," quoth a scout, "and have knives."

While the steamer is puffing to round a great bend,
Does our artist with vigor the coteau ascend;
The warriors perceive him, and quickly prepare
To tender a greeting warm, brilliant, and rare,
And finish the frolic by "lifting his hair."

"How-how!" quoth our artist as rearing his brush,
"Mak-wa" say the warriors as for him they rush;

While seeking to show them his friendship and faith,
They rob him and welt him with jeering and mirth,
Each brave and squaw helping "for all they are worth."

Down hot pours the sun on his shoulders and back,
Each squaw making merry with tickle and whack;
Watch, clothing, and weapons are stripped from his neck,
Squaw, pappoose, and wizard each save from the wreck,
And the breast of the chief, does his locket bedeck.

Lo! modesty shocking, no model so nude
E'er poised for his pencil as for it he stood;
Nor was it on canvas their tracings were quaint,
But the model they tackled with bodkin and paint;
Such greeting by friends! 'twould have ruffled a saint.

On thighs they lizards tattoo in colors bright and true;
On belly plump a bull-boat with naked squaws the crew;
On brawny breast Crow totems of glistening black they
    drew;
On arms and cheek a striping of yellow, red, and blue;
On forehead grinning goblins, all hideous to the view;
And ears and nose fresh eyelets, with gaudy trinkets new,
        Rig up his frontal gear!

Some raven-plumes they plaited among his golden hair,
And eagle-pinions painted across his shoulders fair;
On back a curly bison, with tail erect in air,
With rampant strides was chasing a grizzly to his lair;
Some serpents scaly twining where pants he used to wear,
And pair of wall-eyed owlets where wont to press the
    chair,
        Brought up a brilliant rear!

Sure 'twas a sight that Barnum, with all his craft and gold,
Ne'er saw, or dreamed, or conjured, though half is still
    untold.
A forked post they planted two bison-heads to hold,
And grizzly's head above them, by forked prong con-
    trolled;
With cruel thongs they bound him, as slave in market sold,
And fagots piled around him, lest he was growing cold;
      And then they danced and sung:

      "Si-oux chieftain, tall and bold,
      Maiden fair and wizard old;
      Hun-ka,* weazen, pap-poose† young,
      Warrior with his bow unstrung,
      Meet you, greet you, heart and hand,
      To the secrets of our land,
      And upon your bosom white
      To-tems‡ trace for sacred rite;
      Deep we pierce and bright we paint
      Grizzly bold and bison quaint;
      Shunk-to-ke-cha,§ he-kha-ka,‖
      Shun-ka-wa-kan,¶ wa-pa-ha,**
      Wi-ta-wa-ta,†† sa-pa‡‡ wan,§§
      ‖‖ Wi-chen-yan-na,¶¶ win-i-ban." ***

---

    * Da'-ko-ta, his mother.   † O-jib-wa, Indian child.
    ‡ To'-tems, symbolic Indian name.
    § Da-ko-ta, the other dog, wolf.
    ‖ Da-ko-ta, the antlered male elk.
    ¶ Da-ko-ta, shun-ka, dog; wa-kan, sacred dog, horse.
    ** Da-ko-ta, hat or cap.
    †† Da-ko-ta, ship or boat.   ‡‡ Da-ko-ta, black.
    §§ Da-ko-ta, one, a or an.
    ‖‖ The last line doubtless refers to some maiden of the tribe who had been carried off by the white men.
    ¶¶ Da-ko-ta, girl.   *** O jib-wa, gone.

While wizard circled round him, with pricking thrust of
    spear,
With scalping-knife a warrior carved round his frontal gear,
And hatchet hurled at ear-rings, to test his sense of fear;
Some squaws with rancid bear's-grease his thighs and
    buttocks smear,
In love, with splinters blazing, they singed him there
    and here,
Then kindly fired the fagots, his Indian friends to cheer,
    And then another dance and song:

  "Il-la-hi,* you come to see,
    Lo-lo-lo† you want to be;
    Chit-woot‡ sko-kum,§ bold you come,
    Mos-mos,‖ stupid to your doom,
    Ab-sa-ra-ka,¶ til-la-cume.**
    Que-u-que-u,†† lance and plume,
    Min-ne-ke-wa‡‡ cannot save,
    Min-ne-wa-wa§§ branches wave,
    Kam-ooks‖‖ gaunt around you glare,
    Ka-kaws¶¶ circle in the air.
    By the blood of kindred slain
    Thine shall lance and fagot drain.
    I-san-tan-ka,*** feel our ire,
    Wa-kan-sche-cha,††† in the fire."

---

* Chinook jargon, country our.   † Chinook jargon, conqueror.
‡ Chinook jargon, bear.   § Chinook jargon, brave.
‖ Chinook jargon, buffalo.   ¶ Da-ko-ta, Crow Indian.
** Chinook jargon, enemies.   †† Chinook jargon, circle-circle.
‡‡ Santee, water-god.
§§ Da-ko-ta, pleasant sounds of the breezes in the grove.
‖‖ Chinook jargon, dogs.
¶¶ Chinook jargon, crows or ravens.
*** Da-ko-ta, Big-Knife, American.
††† Da-ko-ta, wa-kan, mystery; sche-cha, bad mystery, devil.

And our confiding artist, what of his faith and love
For persecuted chieftain and loving turtle-dove,
And brood of helpless robins, thrust from their quiet nest?
His feelings still were tender, but—truth must be confessed—
Yearned less for hosts who honored than for their honored guest.

And visions fast are flashing within him and around,
With wonders why he's tattooed and 'mid the fagots bound;
And less he thanked the artists than cursed his coat of paint,
And less his prayers for Indians than execrations quaint,—
Proof that one may die a martyr who still is not a saint.

But lo! the proud steamer is heaving in view,—
"Heap-heap of fine frolic, here goes for one new!
"Wa-wa!"* shouts the wizard, as hurling the brands
And scalping-knife gleaming, quick severs the bands;
From the fire reels our hero, and bewilderingly stands.

The wand of the wizard is wafted amain;
Soon a gantlet-line lengthy is formed on the plain;
Nude chieftain and warrior, buck, pappoose, and squaw,
And curs of all colors, gaunt belly and maw;
Such greeting and parting few guests ever saw!

Alas for our artist! scene lively and quaint,—
But somehow his ardor had vanished for paint,—

---

* Wa-wa', Chinook jargon, a call; as, hear! hear!

And theme for a poet, few better are seen;
But strangely his visions were not with his theme,
But afar with a mother, or the maiden a gleam.

The calliope's trumpet, enlivening, he hears,
And shouts from the steamer, loud greeting with cheers.
One sigh for the maiden he's seeking to find,
One spank from the nude one he's leaving behind,
And into the gantlet he sails like the wind!

Oh, were I a poet to graphic portray
The skill of our bard in the gantlet and fray,—
With switch, knife, or fagot, each pappoose in place,
Each maid with her larrup, and warrior with mace,
To prick, switch, or gash him, then join in the chase.

Faith, never by breech-clouts such running was seen;
Such twisting and turning and dodging between;
Thrusts and blows that were aimed at our hero before
Oft sprawled those behind him in howling and gore;
Sure, his bison helps dodge, and his eagle helps soar.

Soon out of the gantlet he hies him amain,
Leaving yelling pursuers wide-spread o'er the plain;
But the whelps of all sizes, stride, color, and breed,
As wolves swarm around him, ferocious in greed,
Where the Indians are scattered, delaying his speed.

Alack! when with skill he was dodging a brave,
Whose hatchet-blow missed him, and a yelping cur clave,
Another,—not warrior, but cur,—with a yell,
Grabbed his owlets behind, and together they fell,
Dogs, poet, and warriors commingled pell-mell.

But our hero, by doubling in striking the ground,
With somersault double, a leap, and a bound,
Dogs, wizard, and warriors are distanced, and found
On the cactus-thorns sprawling or howling around,
While the war-whoop and scalp-yell redouble the sound !

Nor idle our friends on the steamer, whose gun,
Hurling shell 'mid the warriors, enlivens the fun ;
While calliope-trumpet, screaming whistle, and bell,
The ringing of rifles, the shouting, and yell,
From the stern-paddle steamer commingle and swell !

No greeting to comrades, nor farewell to foes,
Nor brushing of ringlets, nor dusting of clothes ;
No sketching of artist, speech of wizard or seer,—
In plunges our poet,—no river hath fear,—
And steamer he reaches 'mid shouting and cheer.

No mirror he's seeking, no maiden's caress,—
Sure, all laud his running, his swimming, and *dress !*
His greetings as artist and speedy return,
Such lessons of friendship as few ever learn,
And totems of glory as glisten—and burn.

And thus from his sketching our artist returns,
All covered with *glory*, with *bruises*, and *burns ;*
Nor thankful for tokens or totems bestown,—
Though clothing he brought none, his robe is his own,
Nor changing with fashion, nor ever outgrown !

But alas for our poet, scribe, artist, and seer,
The maid of his bosom greets him back with a jeer !

"Oh, where is my locket, with its sweet, smiling face?
For an ugly squaw-bartered breast of breech-clout to
    grace?
Then come ye thus tattooed my fair name to debase?"

And the patrons of science were little less rude;
While Adonis and Venus they worship all nude,
The artist they furnished, who a model returns,
With lofty disdaining their modesty spurns!
Worse than fagots of savage such ingratitude burns!

But just as cash, courage, and patience were gone,
His tattooed form bending, gaunt, famished, and wan,
The tale of his suffering reached Barnum the brave,
Who found him and saved him, and lasting fame gave—
His coat of all colors, "Tattooed, captive, and slave!"

Thus failing untimely as an artist or seer,
And savant and poet,—there is reason to fear,—
His harp with his pencil and scrap-book are flung
Where wizard ne'er tattooed nor poet e'er sung;
Hence these rude strains of tribute, with harp all unstrung,
To the seer and the savage! Adieu, I am done.

THE MOSQUITO.

In eastern vale or western valley
    The stagnant pools his home ;
In northern marsh or warm savanna,
    He welcomes those who roam !

Not Catlin's brush nor Cooper's cunning
    Can paint this insect true,
Nor Shakspeare's Shylock match his dunning,—
    For blood he claims his due.

With fanning wings and music charming,
    Mosquitoes lull their prey,
Safe chance to find, without alarming,
    To steal our blood away.

But in thy fertile vales, Missouri,
    And by the Yellowstone,
Like hornet hordes aroused to fury,
    They greet us to their home.

Sure, 'tis a land of blood and slaughter,
    As many find too true ;
With mud and alkali and water,
    I fear I'm feeling blue !

Bestride my loping steed Deschoteau,
    'Mid antelope on plain,
Or bison herd upon the coteau,
    I'll cheerful feel again.

E'en thus amid life's conflicts ever,
　As day succeeds the night,
Does triumph crown each firm endeavor
　In struggling for the right.

And thou, thou "cussed" little fellow,—
　Blood-sucking leech of prey,—
Rip, roar, and howl, and sing, and bellow!
　"Slap"—takes thy life away!

FRIGHTENED HANS.

A JOLLY Hans, of Olmstead, full, plucky, plump, and strong,
Went prospecting a homestead, and drove his team along;
"Come," quoth he to his *Fraulein*, and to his *kinty Schon*,
"So ven ve pilds der cabin ve alls can help along."

Long, long they chased the sunset o'er prairie, butte, and plain,
To bask in fabled Eden, but everywhere in vain;
Still salter seemed the waters, and shorter grew the grass,
"The shining sands of coteaus reflecting heat like glass.

Weary, faint, and sinking, in misery and woe,
'Mid vision scenes of drinking, where waters never flow,
Mountains! the Rocky Mountains! glad they greet with cheers;
Mirage of gushing fountains dispel their frantic fears.

With joy and hope they rally, and climb the rocky crest;
A glorious smiling valley lay nestling in the West:
"Oh, here will end our sorrow, no further will we roam,
But joyful on the morrow will choose our site for home."

With pail in hand, dismounting, for water for the team,
Hans hastens to the fountain,—oh, horrid stench and steam!

"Zulphur!" he shouts; then stooping, hot, foaming
    water finds,
And hastening from the basin, gets caught in border
    vines.

"Dhrive, *Schon*," he cries, "mein *Sohn!* for zulphur
    sthrong I schmell,
And vater hot mit primstone, for sure ze burning hell
Be's not von mile from dis phlace! Dhrive quick and
    fast, mein Sohn!
Farewell, mein Fraulein Kathrine! Got save mein kinty
    Schon!"

Attached unto the legend is a moral sure as woe:
In scouting a new region, look well before you go.
In vales of stifling brimstone perchance 'tis well to pray,
But glorious greeting geysers—unwise to run away.

Thus sequel sad to legend adheres, as it would seem;
For Hans and John and Fraulein, though safe 'mid
    smoke and steam,
Were captured by the Si-oux in their causeless stampede
    lone;
Fear of scalding led to roasting on the fated Yellow-
    stone.

THE WINDING DELL.

Long o'er the wastes we've wandered,
   Through cactus, sage, and sand;
By lonely watch have pondered
   O'er scenes in native land,—
Of mothers, sires, and brothers,
   Of sisters kind and true,
And fond farewell of lovers,
   As gliding from their view.

And oft the painted savage
   Has flanked our weary way,
On steeds by day to ravage,
   At night with barb to slay;
And blanket-robed, the fallen
   We've hidden 'neath the sod,
With throbbing hearts, then left them
   To solitude—and God!

But in this vale of verdure
   We cease the wastes to roam,
And flocks and herds will nurture
   Around a cabin home,
And soon will end our sorrow
   And wandering in the West,
"Short marching on the morrow
   To gain our park of rest."

THE WINDING DELL.

Thus spake the belted ranger
   Unto his pilgrim sire:
"We're done with tramp and danger"
   Rang round the blazing fire.
Repast of eve is ended,
   The vesper chant is sung;
In cheering carols blended
   Are voice of old and young.

As when the heart is lightest
   Beware of tidings drear,
So when the camp is brightest
   Oh, watch for danger near!
Flash! sharp the rifle, ringing
   Adown the winding dell,
And deadly bullet singing
   To ebbing heart, "Farewell."

And feathered barbs are flying
   Like wintry flakes of snow,
And ghastly forms are lying
   As strewn by torrents flow.
Scant space is found to "cover"
   Around the camp-fire bright,
From foes that round us hover
   In gloom of starless night.

But vengeance speeds the rally
   And mounted gun the boom;
Fast in that lovely valley
   The warrior meets his doom.

And fierce the clang of sabre,
  That tells of deadly stroke;
Strong arm has ceased to labor,
  Proud heart in death is broke.

And many a summer's glory,
  And many a winter's snows,
Shall pass ere fades the story
  Of how these mortal foes
Met in this beauteous valley,
  That swells this winding glen,—
Met, not as maidens dally,
  But quenched their hate like men.

And yet the turf shall brighten
  With verdure where they fell,
And long their bones shall whiten,
  Adown the winding dell.
And ere his race shall wither,
  Or kindred leave the vale,
The red man wandering thither
  Shall still recount the tale.

And yet shall reap the yeoman
  The gladdening sheaves of grain,
Where heart's-blood of the foemen
  Have fertilized the plain.
And yet shall children prattle,
  And yet shall maiden tread
In peace this vale of battle,
  With garlands for the dead.

AFAR FROM THE CITIES AND HAMLETS OF MEN.

[68] Afar from the cities and hamlets of men,
 I follow the streamlet through forest and glen ;
 The elk with proud antlers enlivens the bowers,
 And brilliant and fragrant the meadows with flowers.

 Still onward I wander, till startled by fear,
[69] As thunders from heavens unclouded I hear,
 And rainbows I witness high spanning the walls
 Of cañons deep furrowed by lashing of falls.

 All eager I hasten, entranced by the scene
 Of cataracts double and cascades between,
 And bright-tinted buttress to pinnacles high,—
 Base deep in the cañon, *crest* piercing the sky.

 All heedless of danger, by wild, winding way,
 I haste, 'mid the halos, the thunder, and spray,
[70] Adown to the lichens, mist-nourished and green,
 Where the floods as a deluge from heaven are seen.

 All breathless in efforts of scaling the walls,
 'Mid balsams I press to the head of the falls ;
 And there 'mid the spray on the quivering brink,
 Of the scenes of my childhood, far distant, I think.

 As then, the huge boulders in rolling amain
 I greet with loud shoutings, re-echoed again ;

And cobbles are hurled o'er the swift-rushing stream,
As it glides from my view like a phantom or dream.

Then along the wild rapids, by cedars o'erhung,
Where artist ne'er pencilled nor bird ever sung,
And flood-gates of torrents from mountains of snow
Are echoing beside me above and below.

And here in this grotto deep-sheltered and warm,
All weary I slumber, unheeding the storm,
Whose thunders deep-rumbling commingle again
With the spray of the waters whence gathers the rain.

No clouds fleck the terrace, no winds reach the glen,
When to life and its struggles I waken again,
And pensively ponder o'er scenes that are fled,
Of hopes that are vanished, of friends who are dead.

And life's panorama drear passes along,
Mist-phantoms commingled of sorrow and song,
Alluring each promise, but failure attends,—
Foes only are steadfast, inconstant are friends.

Unselfish I've struggled to benefit men,
Regretless I leave them, my refuge the glen,
Where mist-nourished flowers and carpets of green
Commingling in bowers like Eden are seen.

"Henceforth be my music the cataract's roar
My refuge the grotto, to leave nevermore;
Light halos encircling my winding-sheet be,
A tomb be the pool of this grotto for me,
And the rainbow my pathway of spirit set free!

OH, IS THERE IN THIS WORLD SO DREAR?

Oh, is there in this world so drear
    A scene of harrowing pain
Like haunts of those to memory dear
    We ne'er shall meet again?

[72] In crumbling home of friends afar
    The wolf and vulture dwell,
And screams and howls deriding mar
    The scenes once loved so well.

[73] Above the ceaseless dash and roar,
    Where mountain torrents greet,
The famished eagles circling soar,
    And fierce coyoutas meet.

And, all unbidden, memory turns
    To bloody scenes again,
And only slumbering ire burns
    With vengeance for the slain.

And throbbing heart instinctive swells,
    And surging pulse is wild,
As weapons gleam whose ringing knells
    Count coups* on race defiled.

Will tourist yet who safely roams
    With buoyant hope and tread,
Flowers pluck amid the bleaching bones
    Of us, the unknown dead?

---

* Scalps.

And will the bards here yet to sing
   Know aught or care for those
Whose music was the rifle's ring,
   And couch the mountain snows?

Who oft alone in mountain glen,
   Or bands in valley strife,
As heroes lived, and died as men
   Who dearly sell their life?

Oh, is there land of peace and rest
   For wanderers below,
Where yet the weary shall be blest,
   Where soothing waters flow?

Where reunite the mountain band,
   Where each shall know a friend?
And dwell for aye in Mystic-Land,
   Where kindred spirits blend?

Ah, yes, ah, yes, such land and home,
   Such rest and kindred shore!
Where friends shall greet, and foes may come,
   But meet as foes no more!

TO THE TIE AT HOME.

Oh, thou who dreads my starting,
    Far o'er the West to roam,
Whose tears endear our parting,
    Whose smiles allure me home!

[74] Far away on the cliffs of this wild roaring river,
    I remember the rill near the cot of my bride;
Home-trail with that bride through the wild-wood together
    On our morning of union, of hope, and of pride.

Of the long years of toil and of hardships together,
    Rude tomb of our first-born, in the forest alone;
Fond hopes o'er the fair locks of those we thought never
    Would eager forsake us for strangers unknown.

Of the dark days of war, of bloodshed and sorrow,
    When thou girded my sword with a tear and a prayer
That from the fierce strife and the carnage of morrow
    I safe might return to thy fond arms so fair.

In the halls of my country, when the conflict was o'er,
    Thy soft cheeks were blooming with pride and with love
For him thou dreamed fondly would leave thee no more
    Till called to sweet rest in the mansions above.

But the years have rolled onward, our children are gone;
   Time has blighted our vision, our thin locks are gray;
In a far distant region I'm weary and 'lorn;
   As the dew of the morning earth's hopes fade away.

Oh, bright through the cedars the visions that steal,
   The light-circling halos ascending in spray;
Oh, pathway is this to the land o' the leal?
   And life, as these waters, thus gliding away?

Yet, loved one to me, thou art still ever young;
   All rosy thy cheeks and bright beaming thine eye;
When pale are these roses, life's harp sleeps unstrung.
   In the green groves of Eden, oh, meet me! Good-by!

THE WARRIOR'S GRAVE.

FAINT wane the hopes of loved ones
  To greet their honored dead;
Chill howl the storms of winter
  Around his mountain bed.

Fierce scream the wolf and raven
  Around the vacant grave;
Earnest the search of comrade
  For relics of the brave.

[75] A mould'ring plate and headboard,
  Carved on the field of gore
By sword of faithful comrade,—
  His name and date,—no more.

These records, faint but truthful,
  Tell where he fell and died;
Commingling bones of foeman
  Bleach on the mountain-side.

Through mountain gorge and tempest,
  By ancient friend alone,
These relics of our hero
  Were borne to friends who moan.

Is this meet tomb for hero
  On countless fields of strife?
And this reward for yielding
  Home, happiness, and life?

'Tis not a realm of justice,
  Nor yet of Eden's bowers;
Too oft of wrong and suffering,
  This cruel world of ours.

Oh, rather choose the sharing
  A humble home of love,
And wisely there preparing
  For Eden's bowers above!

I SING IN SONGS.

I SING in songs of gliding lays
Of forest scenes in border days;
Of rippling rills in valleys green,
And mirrored hills in lakelet sheen;
Of mountain-peaks begirt with snow,
And flowery parks, pine-girt below;
Of daring deeds of border braves,
On dashing steeds, to gory graves;
Of brawny breast, 'neath painted plume,
On warrior's crest, in dash to doom;
Of light canoe on dashing shore,
And daring crew, who'll row no more;
Of goblins grim and cañons grand,
And geysers spouting o'er the strand;
Of Mystic Lake, of Wonder-Land;

And of a youth, from humble home,
To parents' help, impelled to roam
O'er prairies green or thirsty plain,
Or dashing streams, that mountains drain;
And far away 'mid snows to roam,
To morsel furnish those at home;
To manhood grown, leaves border life,
Prepares a home and seeks a wife;
Then in the camp or council pure,
On side of justice ever sure,
Till age has silvered o'er his head,—
Old comrades gone and loved ones dead,—

Still, as the oak, leafless and shorn,
Amid a forest, rent and torn,
Still cheerful waiting for the day
From earthly cares to pass away,
With life well spent, and promise plain
That losing earth he'll heaven gain.

BLAZE BRIGHTLY, O CAMP-FIRE!

BLAZE brightly, O camp-fire! beneath the dark pines,
While sadly the hunter 'mid trophies reclines.
Blow blithely, O zephyrs! from sweet-scented vales,
To blending untimely in moaning and wails,
'Mid snow-crested mountains in fierce howling gales.

How oft, 'neath the branches of cedars low bent,
Or clustering balsams, for refuge intent,
Have I, when benighted in fast-falling snow,
Found shelter and comfort by camp-fire aglow
That none but a climber of mountains can know!

And there have I pondered, all pensive and lone,
On days that are vanished, on hopes that have flown.
My birthplace a cottage in warm flowery grove,
Kind parents and brothers and sisters to love,
And Bible and Sabbaths to point me above.

All peaceful my slumbers, all happy my home;
No visions of dangers, no longings to roam;
An Eden in promise, no Eden to prove,
But a thorn with a rosebud, a blighting in love,
And far from that Eden I wander and rove.

All slowly but surely time passes away;
'Neath willows low bending friends mingle with clay;

Uncounted, in circles the seasons have fled;
Unnoticed, these tresses are bleaching my head;
Unconscious, I'm nearing the rest of the dead.

Howl, tempest! befitting, the thunders that roll,
This turmoil in bosom, this quaking of soul.
A long life reviewing of folly and pain,
All bubbles its pleasures, its struggles in vain,
⁷⁶ Earth's treasures all vanished, no heaven to gain.

UNION OF THE VALLEYS.

Where the broad, romantic valley of the dashing Yellowstone
Greets Missouri's turbid waters, far toward the setting sun,
Where the Man-dan and the Te-ton, with the Yank-ton and the Crow,
And the bloody Black-foot Pe-gan, with the British Knis-te-naux,
Meet in battle on the war-horse, or in bull-boat float at ease,
There was built the stockade "Union," a mart of fur amid the Rees.

Long around that distant station gathered rovers of the plain,
White and red, of every nation, such as ne'er shall meet again;
[77] For the ever-fickle river veered away to meet its mate,
[78] And the fort, its cache and lodges, were abandoned to their fate.
Garnered scenes, by sketch of Stanley, Catlin's brush, or Irving's pen,
Of trappers true and voyageurs, alone survive those daring men.

Now again the painted warrior, 'mid the ruins of the past,
Builds his teepee and his earth-lodge, master of the site at last.

Sweet and pleasant is the memory of our youthful friends and braves;
Sad and lonely 'tis to wander o'er their foe-betrodden graves;
But the ever-restless white man savage tribes can ne'er withstand;
Soon the pale-face race shall conquer and possess that alley land.

Then, perchance, o'er graves of comrades whom the painted savage slew
Cypress boughs and wreaths of laurel shall entwine o'er warriors true.
[79] Oh, for bard to chant their requiem! Oh, for storied pen to save
From the silence of oblivion legends of the true and brave!
Like the union of these valleys, may their spirits meet and blend!
Like these waters, ever gliding, may their happiness ne'er end!

OH, FOR BARD TO TRULY TREASURE!

⁸⁰ OH, for bard to truly treasure
    Border scenes of days agone!
And in strains of thrilling measure
    Garner deeds else soon unknown,
    Forest scenes ere long o'ergrown!

Now of daring deeds of yeomen
    Round their cabins in the wilds,
Then of voyageurs when the foemen,
    By their ever crafty guiles,
    Drove them to the distant isles!

As of Hans along the Hudson,
    Then the wild Manhattan shore,—
Now a mart of matchless splendor,
    That no cloud in passing o'er
    Mirrored in the days of yore.

Thus, perchance, the haunt of trappers,
    Or the gulch where miners dwell,
Searching for the hidden treasures,
    Shall for toil reward them well,
    And the wealth of nations swell.

Even thus the bard in singing
    Strains of those who fighting fell
By the bolts from rifles ringing,
    For himself may harvest well,
    And the works of knowledge swell.

RUSTIC BRIDGE AND CRYSTAL FALLS.

[81] WILL these feet that trip so lightly
    O'er this structure rude but strong,
Or these eyes which beam so brightly,
    E'er greet scenes more meet for song?

Skipping rill from snowy fountains
    Dashing through embow'red walls,
Fairy dell 'mid frowning mountains,
    Grotto pool and Crystal Falls.

Charming dell, begirt with wonders,
    Mighty falls on either hand,
Quiet glen amid their thunders,
    Matchless, save in Wonder-Land.

O'er their mingled mists and shadows
    Rainbows beauteous, tinted, rise,
And their ever-changing halos
    Blend and vanish in the skies.

Shy beneath the crystal waters,
    In the grotto of the glen,
Sylvan forms of nature's daughters
    Sport and bathe unseen by men.

RUSTIC BRIDGE AND CRYSTAL FALLS.

Here we part, perchance forever,
 In our pilgrimage below;
Yet in scenes like this together,
 Above may we each other know!

HIGH TOWERS THE CRAGGY SUMMIT.

High towers the craggy summit, begirt with glistening snow,
Mirrored in emerald lakelets in flowery vales below;
Proud soars the fearless eagle around the frozen crest,
Low, 'mid the blooming daisies, the turtle builds her nest;
Down verdant sloping terrace flow sweetly gliding rills,
Roars cataract like thunder in echoes 'mid the hills;
The woolly-sheep and big-horn trail deep in mountain snow,
[82] And beavers build their wick-e-ups where warm the waters flow.

[83] Gigantic wrecks of forests, all fossilized to stone,
By trailing vines and cedars are, trellis-like, o'ergrown;
Through flowery vales the river meanders on its way
To cataract and cañon, their thunder, mist, and spray;
And vales of blooming roses are sheltered deep and warm
Amid the towering mountains, where howls the Alpine storm;
With zephyr-hiss, the ripples glide laughing to the shore,
Where tempest-driven billows terrific dash and roar!

In all these blooming valleys, along each crystal stream,
And snow-encircled lakelet, where quivering halos gleam,
These labyrinths of goblins, and spouting geysers grand,
Unnumbered are the marvels throughout the Wonder-Land;

As wintry storms build snow-fields, and summer breezes
    thaw,
⁸⁴ All nature seems in contrast, in beauty, size, or awe,—
Creation, growth, and *ruin,* the universal law !

LONELY GLEN.

[85] 'Tis lion's scream resounding
　　Adown the lonely glen,
Like those once here astounding,
　　From throats of savage men;
When angry rifle ringing,
　　And scorching sulphur smoke,
And deadly bullet singing,
　　The luring silence broke!

Plumed warriors fierce and savage,
　　With hatchet, lance, and knife,
The camp of tourist ravage,
　　And seek the owner's life;
Too late is flight for safety,
　　And fight with savage vain,—
Soon crimson rill joins torrents
　　That snowy mountains drain!

Are these the brands of camp-fire?
　　And theirs this battered plate?
From wounded here the death-cry,
　　For mercy came too late!
Yes, but the day is dawning
　　Athwart the morning star,
To saddle fast, a warning,
　　For duty calls afar.

REYNOLDS'S DIRGE.

OH, know ye the coteaus and valleys between,
The rose-tinted bowers and meadows of green,
And pure crystal river, from mountains of snow,
Encrimsoned by carnage that curdled its flow
With steeds and their riders, and foemen in strife,
Commingled and falling 'neath hatchet and knife?
And the rose on the coteau was tinted again
With crimson fast spouting from wounds of the slain,
When Custer led phalanx of heroes as bold
As the Greeks or the Romans in legends of old
To ambush and slaughter, and mourning in homes
Afar from where tempests are bleaching their bones.

I've trailed o'er that coteau and roamed o'er that plain;
In that valley built camp-fire 'mid bones of the slain.
[86] My fagots were ruins of teepee and tent,
'Mid war-robes and blankets all gory and rent.
There at eve came the spirit of Charley the bold,
Not gory, but blooming, the hero of old,
And this was his greeting: "All welcome, my friend!
The clay thou art seeking has gone with the wind;
My few bones remaining by the willow so lone
Take homeward returning to rest with thine own.
But birthplace or kindred cease efforts to trace,—
The hatchet has slaughtered the last of my race."

YES, BE IT THUS.

Yes, be it thus; the die is cast,
  The fatal word is spoken;
The halo-cloud of charming past
  And chain of bondage broken.
Oh, 'mid the gloom of coming years,
  Will dreams of friends forsaken,
Or shrunken cheeks, too dry for tears,
  Remorse or shame awaken?

Will visions then of happy days
  In snow-girt park or valley,
And cheering dreams of camp-fire blaze,
  And loving song and sally,
Blend sweet with those of wavy brow,
  Where pledges fair were riven,
And quivering lips renew the vow
  To meet again in heaven?

IN CABIN, CAMP, OR COUNCIL.

[87] In cabin, camp, or council, in husbandry or war,
In sunny native valleys or snowy mountains far,
Two kindred spirits blended, alike their acts and aims,—
Their earthly duties ended, together find their names.
Mount Washburn and Mount Norris like battlements arise;
O'er cataract and cañon their summits pierce the skies;
Path-seeker and path-maker, personified to stand,
Enduring guide for tourists throughout the "Wonder-Land."

YES, EVERY ONE A MAN.

I've trailed the proud Missouri
   Till fountain rill I stride,
And founts of the Missoula,
   Adown the sunny side;
Till countless rills in blending
   A mighty river form,
And from the Hell-Gate Cañon
   I greet a valley warm.

And here a town I enter,
   A shoeing shop and mill,
A tavern in the centre,
   And corral on the hill;
A score of earth-roofed cabins,
   A rum and gambling lair,
John Chinaman and laundry,
   And teepees here and there.

And lo! a belted ranger,
   A chum in days of yore,
Shouts, "Well, how are you, stranger?
   Let's shake your paw once more."
Full soon we drank to courage,
   And loud the toast and song,
And glasses quaffed to comrades
   Far o'er the mountains gone.

And in the morn we ramble
    Beside a mountain rill,
Till silent camp we enter
    Upon a sunny hill;
And here we halt to ponder
    Beside each turfy home
Of those who're done with wandering,
    Of those who've ceased to roam.

And here we gaze in silence
    Upon the hillocks green,
The moaning pines and balsams,
    And brilliant flowers between,
Until my ancient comrade,
    With quivering lip and breath,
Recalls each name and story,
    And manner of his death.

"Beneath this branched cedar
    Sleeps comrade true and brave,
Who ever trod the war-path
    The innocent to save;
But as the rescuing seaman
    Oft sinks beneath the wave,
So Harry fell for others,
    And here's his lowly grave.

"Here's Ned, the daring trapper
    Along the Yellowstone,
Who scaled the snowy mountains,
    And gulches trod alone;
But while he trapped the beaver,
    To sell his coat so fair,

The Bannocks trailed the trapper
    Unto his brushy lair,
And here his bones are mould'ring,
    While they retain his hair.

"Here's Jack and Bill, the brothers,
    Who left a happy home,
And loving friends and sweethearts,
    The western wilds to roam
In search of gold and romance
    But trailed and toiled in vain;
While bravely fighting Koot-nays*
    Were numbered with the slain,
And their bleaching bones we gathered
    Along the Cœur d'Alène.†

"When melting snows were foaming
    Adown the Blackfoot Gorge,
En route from winter's roaming,
    Encamped was daring George
Upon a narrow terrace,
    Beneath its rocky walls,
Whence icy waters swept him
    Relentless o'er the falls.

"Upon the roaring Loo-Loo,
    In howling wintry storm,
Nor fire nor tent nor teepee,
    Or robe to keep them warm,
These brothers braved the tempest
    Till chilled was curdling tide,
Then robed in snowy blankets,
    Together clasped they died.

---

* Indians of the Koot-e-nay tribe.
† Pronounced cor-de-lane.

"Nor least, but last and saddest,
  The fate of comrades here,
Who closed a drinking frolic
  Around a bloody bier;
And then their wrathful comrades,
  As vigilants arrayed,
O'er forked pine threw lasso,
  And in a noose each swayed,
And sadly 'neath these willows
  In morn these three were laid.

"Ah, yes, their vigils keeping,
  Above the torrent's roar,
Each peacefully is sleeping,
  All here the twenty-four,
All here in glory lying,
  From foe no coward ran,
Each spur and booted dying,
  Yes, every one a man!"

THE ARTIST STANLEY.

O ARTIST! true artist! who far in the West,
O'er coulee and coteau and bleak mountain-crest,
'Mid Mo-doc and Man-dan, Brule, Black-foot, and Crow,
Bronzed teepee and totem, lance, quiver, and bow!

O painter! who painted o'er prairie and plain
The lodge of the living, the cairn of the slain,
Proud plume of the warrior, and maiden so shy,
And prisoner firm-bound 'mid the fagots to die!

O limner! bold limner! on war-trail or street,
On moor or on mountain no more shall we meet;
Thy paintings portray thee more life-like than song,
More valued and lauded as time glides along!

O Stanley! brave Stanley! thy rambles are o'er,
And brush laid aside,—thou wilt need it no more!
[88] But "Uncas" and "War-path" and "Signal" shall stay.
When thy head, heart, and hand have long moulder'd away.

O Eden! pure Eden! sweet home of the blest,
Where the brave and the loving in harmony rest,
May painter and poet in ecstasy blend
With saints and with angels in bliss without end!

MIN-NE-HA-HA.

BREEZES briskly blowing,
Waters brightly flowing,
　Thine, Min-ne-ha-ha.
Warriors bold are banished,
Maidens dusky vanished,
　From Min-ne-ha-ha.
Another race are sowing,
Or with chariots mowing,
Lovely cities growing,
　Round Min-ne-ha-ha.
Until time be ended
Be thy beauties blended,
　Sweet Min-ne-ha-ha!

LOVELY RIVER.

Flow on, thou lovely river!
   Go smiling on thy way,
And gathered floods deliver,
   In thunder, mist, and spray,
Amid the arching rainbows,
   High o'er the triple falls,
Where quivering mystic halos
   Bright tint the cañon walls.

E'en thus may life, in gliding
   Adown the stream of time,
Glean wealth and worth abiding
   From many a sunny clime.
Nor soul on brink to shiver,
   But boldly launch away,
Joyous to meet its Giver
   In realms of radiant day.

BURIAL TEEPEE.

Amid the Judith Bad Lands, beside the Mussel-shell,
[89] The Ab-sa-ra-ka chieftain most bravely fighting fell;
Fighting the Si-oux savage, to save his pale-face friend,
His list of gallant battles came to a glorious end.

When the bloody strife was ended, and weapons ceased
    to gleam
Within the snowy cañon and along the sunny stream,
  'Mid reeking scalps of foemen, lashed to his steed of
    foam,
In triumph sad they bore him unto his silent home.

In gorgeous war-tent teepee once captured from his foes,
  He's near Camp Lewis sleeping, in dreamless, sweet
    repose,
  With lance and cross o'er doorway, rich trophies there
    abound,
  With Black-feet scalps above him, and Si-oux scalps
    around;

To-tems of saint and savage, of white man and of red,
In brilliant colors painted above the mighty dead;
There let him rest in triumph, and moulder into dust,
His spirit's with Wa-kan-da, on whom he set his trust.

BOLD TRAPPER OF THE CAMP-FIRE.

⁹⁰ Bold trapper of the camp-fire
 In thy daring days of youth,
Meek Christian when a grandsire
 On the homeward trails of truth.

Proud rover of the mountains,
 Scaled thou oft the snowy crest;
In vale of emerald fountains
 Lowly is thy couch of rest.

Thy war-path days are ended,
 Ranch in heaven's park begun;
There may our trails be blended,
 And our camps and comrades one!

THE WARRIOR'S DIRGE.

[91] Gone, brave brother, gone from the suffering and strife,
Commencing with birth, only ending with life;
Through the red fields of war spared in safety to roam,
Life's duties all o'er, rest with loved ones at home.

May thy myrtle-wreaths won in the blooming of youth,
In the halls of the schools or the chapels of truth,
Entwine with the laurel-bays earned on the field,
Where glory is carved by the sabre's bold wield!

And who are thy friends in the land o' the leal,
The warriors in mail, with their helmets of steel,—
A Wallace, a Bruce, or an archer, as Tell,
In triumph who lived, or in victory fell?

And still dost thou view, on the coteau or plain,
Charge of golden-haired chief to the carnage again;
And thy comrades, alas! all lifeless and lorn,
Asleep where they fought, 'mid the cactus and thorn?

And view ye the reapers, with carbine and sword,
In the field of war-bonnets and plumes by the ford;
And the riderless steeds, careering again,
O'er the thick-scattered sheaves on the harvest of slain?

Avaunt with such deeds by the dwellers of earth!
The grim scenes of war, or its revels and mirth!
Far better the acts and the mansions of those
Who pruning-hooks make of the spears of their foes

Ho, signal the giants of carnage and gain!
Come, spend ye a night with the ghosts of your slain!
Then turn, if ye will, to your slaughter and lust,
Brief heyday of revel, then moulder in dust.

And where the immortal, the God-given soul?
Its mansion eternal, is heaven its goal,
Or sinks it in sorrow with spirits akin,
Their sharers in crime and the heralds of sin?

Oh, better the reapers with sickles of right,
Who cleave for the gleaners of freedom and light;
And as sheaves from the harvest they bring at its close,
Bright bundles of friends they have won of their foes.

Soul-cheering the hope of a land far away,
And the reveille call at the dawn of the day,
When the heroes of earth shall immortal ascend,
With laurels bedecked and where angels attend.

CYPRESS SHADOWS.

[92] "Where the long reeds quiver, where the pines make
    moan,
By the forest river sleeps our babe alone."
Thus a yearning mother, in a flowery grove,
Seeks her sobs to smother with a chant of love:
"England's field-flowers blooming may not deck his grave;
Cypress shadows, looming o'er him, darkly wave."

"Far away we journeyed from our native land,
O'er the briny ocean, o'er the burning sand;
For my loved ones hoping, thus I wandered far,
Hence this loving bosom bears a cureless scar.
'Neath the pine-tops moaning, in his lowly grave,
Leave I a pledge of heaven, other gems to save.

"In my weary wanderings to a land afar,
In my camp-fire visions will a twinkling star,
'Mid the waving shadows, smiling sweet and fair,
From the azure heavens, guide me where you are,—
Not this tomb so lowly, where the shadows lie,
But in regions holy, far beyond the sky?

"Hence, in wanderings dreary in the mighty West,
When my way is weary and my heart oppressed,
As I count my jewels, shall this shining star
Fill the broken circlet, and guide me where you are,—
Not beneath the cypress, 'mid the forest gloom,
But in bowers of Eden, bright with love and bloom?"

I'VE TRAILED THE PROUD COLUMBIA.

I'VE trailed the proud Columbia, from fountain-head in snows,
To where the bold Shoshone through lava-desert flows;
Have crossed the pass St. Regis and lake of Cœur d'Alène,
The lovely glades of Camas and lava-girt Spokane;
Have searched the lovely grottos, and scaled their rugged walls,
And traced the Peluse turbid unto its sacred falls.

[93] And here I pause and ponder at trace of friend of old,
An orphan left to wander before the days of gold.
A home he found in teepee of Spokane chieftain true,
And rollicked with the kam-ooks,* and as a pappoose grew;
With squaws he dug the camas, the maize he learned to grind,
And strode the loping pinto, with naked squaw behind.

Nor aught knew he of kindred, nor cared he for his race,
Until his form expanded and bearded grew his face.
"Than water blood is thicker" is proverb old and true,
And thus his race he cherished in seeking comrades new;
And when the blazing signal, from mountain-crest afar,
Warned him of bloody onset and unrelenting war
By friends of his adoption against those of his birth,
With parting kiss to sister, he boldly sallied forth.

---

* Kam'-ooks, dogs.

In vain the war-whoop ringing roused warriors to his trail;
Nor deadly bullet singing, nor loping steeds prevail.
His pinto through the valley far led them in the chase,
Then swam the Umatilla, and proudly won the race;
Nor checked his foaming charger till in his youth and pride,
Beneath the flag of Steptoe, he fought as scout and guide.

Full soon the conflict opens upon Columbia's plain,
And in the mountain valleys that foaming torrents drain;
Nor time to let the story of fighting, fierce and long,
'Twixt those who fought for glory and those who, doubly strong,
Fought in their native valleys, fought o'er their fathers' graves,
Fought by their blazing teepees, and 'mid their dying braves,
Chose death in gory blankets to life as cringing slaves.

Thus back they hurled the pale-face when Steptoe's fight was o'er,
And to the Peluse sacred their trail was red with gore.
That weary moons the remnant they sorely did invest,
With famished pinto rations those bleaching bones attest;
And only for the salmon that crowd the narrow stream,
No pale-face from that cañon would living e'er been seen;
For lo! an old tradition of generations gone
Declared the salmon sacred below the falls to spawn,
Till, lest the sacred fishes should feed the foe they fear,
The Chenooks check their running with brushy dam and weir.

Oft in his pangs of hunger our youth would hear from
  those
He left in hour of danger to aid their mortal foes.
When from the cliff the chieftain, at eve when all was
  still,
Would ring the clarion war-whoop in echoes from the
  hill,
With taunting jeers, "Ho, Sko-kum!* ho, traitor Til-la-
  koom!†
Your Il-li-hu‡ you're viewing, and soon you'll meet your
  doom!
Ho, reared ye in my teepee, you knave in long-knife hire!
You traitor to my children, you soon shall feel my ire,
In running of the gantlet or roasting in the fire!

"But lest your death be speedy, a morsel choice I give;
For while I'm reaping vengeance I want you still to live,"
As the shank of a cay-ou-ta, or skull of car-a-bou,
Or putrid head of salmon, with jeering taunt he threw,
Then strode away in triumph, to gloat o'er insult new.

Blend with his steps receding on the air of evening still,
From an overhanging cedar, the voice of whippoorwill,
In accents low and mournful, as widowed turtle-dove,
"Oh, list, my foster-brother! oh, hear, my truant love!
For you my heart is breaking!" in accents low and mild;
It was the voice of Noo-na, the chieftain's darling child.

"Why left ye thus our teepee? why went ye thus astray?
And from my arms in breaking you tore my heart away.

---

* Sko'-kum, brave.   † Til'-la-koom, enemy.   ‡ Il'-li-hu', country.

Oh, live you not for vengeance my sire declares your due,
But for your foster-sister, your Noo-na, ever true!"
Then sack of choicest viands from towering cliff she threw,
And ere his blessings reached her had vanished from his view.

Scarce need to tell the sequel. In every age and clime
The daring deeds of lovers was ever theme sublime.
Amid the scenes that follow, of carnage on the plain,
Escaped the daring ranger and the maiden of Spokane,
And in a hidden valley this ranger yeoman tills;
Soon bounteously the harvests their bridal teepee fills,
And rollick on the pintos their brood of whippoorwills.

HO, WAKEN!

⁹⁴ Ho, waken, you dwellers in chambers of clay,
Arise from your slumbers and welcome the day!
Come forth from your prison, flesh, raiment, and arms,
And greet us with welcome, no needless alarms.

We're only your brothers from over the sea,
Thus rending your fetters and setting you free ·
Stalk forth as the warriors and sorcerers bold,
And greet us with music and legends of old.

Whose flesh-covered bones strode forth as a brave
In the battle-axe combat? Who's cringed as a slave?
And here are their mothers one moaning for those
Who came not again from the banquet of foes.

⁹⁵ And whose is this dust in these chambers beside?
Mingled ashes of those who as patriots died,
At the stake on the coteau of far-distant plain,
Or the torrents of gore in the vale of the slain?

Or are they the ashes of sacrifice grand
To the gods in the fires of a priest-ridden land,
Where mothers oft gave, under wizard control,
The fruit of the womb for the weal of the soul?

And how came these shells from the deep-rolling waves
Of an ocean afar to these prairie land graves?

And what were the viands that in them was given
To nourish the soul in its journey to heaven?

⁹⁶ And why are these ramparts so lofty and long
Widespread o'er the plains where the antelope throng,
With the deer, elk, and beaver, and elephant grand,
All trailing in earth to a sunnier land?

Whence came ye? Where wandered? Or perished you
    here?
As a race are ye dwelling where proud forests rear
Their shafts and their branches defying the gales,
O'er a people asleep in their own native vales.

No answer, no greeting, nor motion nor moans;
Your dwellings still crumble, still moulder your bones;
Thus careful I glean from this chamber of clay
These relicts for science in halls far away.

And the remnant I carefully cover again,
Then mournfully hie to the valley or plain,
Sad traces to find in the cairns of the dead
Of a race who for ages uncounted have fled.

All pensive I muse of those relicts of yore,
The labors of those who shall labor no more,
Then wondering turn to the monuments grand
Of the race that now governs this cairn-dotted land.

When ages uncounted shall circle again,
And this race of proud vandals shall sleep with the slain,
O'er their crumbling ruins of iron and stone
May wander the warriors of races unknown.

NORTHERN CLIME.

⁹⁷ Faint I recall, through mists of time,
The thrilling scenes of Northern clime:
The outward voyage in birch canoe,
As home and friends recede from view;
Then long blue Huron's pine-clad shore,
And great Superior's waters roar,
Lake of the Wilds, and penance beg
For cursing gnats on Winnepeg;
And then with buoyant hope and song,
With pole and paddle firm and strong,
Ascend thy floods, Sas-Katch-a-wan.

Long are the days, but circles low
The orb of warmth on crests of snow,
Which tower athwart its slanting rays,
And seem at eve with gold ablaze,
Until retinged with mellow light
By silvery rays from orb of night,
Which o'er deep cañons dim at noon
Oft soars the brilliant "harvest moon,"—
As fair as in our distant home;—
To cheer us as we toiling roam,
And gild the dangers yet to come.

Oh, these brilliant days are waning, and bitter nights
    begun
With the fading moons of autumn and the sinking of
    the sun;

Soon all the narrow valleys wear blankets white of snow,
And icy cinches* hamper the mountain-torrents' flow;
Canoes are left for sledges, and shaggy kam-ooks strong
By thong are driven tandem to haul our goods along.
And thus we northward journey among the Knis-te-neaux,
In trapping of the beaver or slaying car-a-bou,
Or trading beads and blankets, or gaudy trinkets new,
For martin pelts, or otter, and foxes white or blue,
Till on the Ath-a-bas-can we build a stockade new.

Soon our Norwegian snow-shoes we carve of sapling long,
Or cunning weave the web-foot of moose-wood bark and
    thong,
Then bold in winter's twilight, o'er drifting fields of
    snow,
We trail the fox and shun-ka and trotting car-a-bou,
Or 'mid the cedar thickets or stinted balsams green,
The moose, the shaggy musk-ox, or crafty wolverine,
And of their coats we fashion huge outer garments warm,
Or 'neath them, rolled in blankets, defy the Arctic storm,
Or watch the wavy halos athwart the "Northern Pole,"
With icy fingers clasping to tear away the soul,
The while their matchless splendors o'er all the heavens
    roll.

When from such scenes returning, with weary limbs we
    come,
And by the fagots burning enjoy our wintry home,
In vigils long and soothing in place of slumbers gone,
When, as the night-watch shivering, we swell our muscles
    wan,
Then cheerful join the frolics dismissing fear and care,
On snow-shoes trail the ermine or fight the polar bear,

---

* Cinches, Spanish, saddle-girths.

Until the sun returning from lengthened wintry night
Reflects from icy spangles its countless gleams of light,
With joyous shouts of welcome that Arctic night is past,
As monks from fasting penance rejoin in grand repast,
And shout and song and legend around our blazing fires,
The Cree, the Brule, and Briton, and sons of Pilgrim sires;
And oft, when storms are howling, join in the circling dance
The brawny lads of Scotland, with kilt and plume askance,
The jolly heirs of Erin, and merry sons of France.

    These scenes are o'er, bright visions fled
    Shall meet no more,—the actors dead.
    Alas! their graves are scattered wide
    From mountain-crest to ocean-tide;
    Some sleep in vaults in Christian lands,
    Uncoffined some in desert sands;
    Some fell in deadly border strife
    By piercing barb or gleaming knife;
    Some far from friends, who ne'er shall know
    Where curdling life-tides ceased to flow,
    In winding-sheet of Alpine snow;
    Some for their country fought and fell,
    In victory shouting, "All is well!"
    The booming gun their funeral knell,
    And coming bards their fame shall swell;
    Lone one, as bough of mistletoe,
    Clings still to life amid the snow;
    May melting torrents here below
    Strand him where Eden's streamlets flow!

DE SOTO.

[98] Damp was the day and dreary, the night was dark and cold;
Worn were my limbs and weary, my refuge hovel old;
While Christmas bells were jingling in merry distant home,
Rife was the night with revels where duty called to roam.
'Twas by the Mississippi, where ancient cypress rear
Above the sluggish bayous the pendent mosses drear,
With fevered brow and throbbing, I dreamed or seemed to dream
Of stifled moan and wailing, and flickering torch's gleam;
A group of grizzled warriors around a mossy bed,
And priests their masses chanting for the spirit of the dead.
It was the proud De Soto, by toil and sorrow slain,
And his comrades with Pizarro, the cavaliers of Spain.

Dim through the shadows o'er them, back rolls the tide of time,
Till plumed and mounted warriors, they leave their native clime,
And 'neath its floating banners embark upon the main,
Far in the western Indies to gold and glory gain.
Balmy the laughing breezes that swell their eager sails;
Eden the land which greets them, of mountains, hills, and dales;

Peaceful the chief who meets them upon Peruvian shore;
Patient the faithful toilers, who bounteous harvests store;
Fatal the hour that taught them to wash its golden sand;
Christians, the men who slew them with sabre, spear, and
    brand;
Brazen the thanks to Heaven for gold with gory stain
By these comrades of Pizarro, these cavaliers of Spain.

When from the land of Incas they greet its placid shore,
Broad looms their trail of plunder, of revelry and gore;
And of the winds uniting to swell their waiting sails,
Laden the mountain breezes with a slaughtered nation's
    wails.
And when the pillaged Eden recedes beneath the waves,
Nameless the scenes of revel with shackled female slaves.
In narrow land 'twixt oceans, like worthless lemon-rind,
As feast for famished vultures, the weak are left behind.
To Spanish isles they visit, as conquerors they come,
And loud the shouts of greeting, the trumpet, fife, and
    drum;
And thus as Christian warriors they leave the raging
    main,
And seek their native valleys, these conquerors from Spain.

Alas! the shameful story of banquets long and grand,
And badges bright of glory from prince of native land.
And oft the thanks to Heaven, and loud the praise of
    those
Who crossed the raging ocean to "conquer pagan foes;"
While to the priests in masses, for fallen comrades' souls,
Pile high Peruvian plunder and Mexican pistoles;
And proudly-titled maidens caress the cheeks of those
Dark-bronzed in scorching deserts, or scarred in fighting
    foes.

Then from their prince and Heaven a title good and grand
Is to De Soto given for realm in distant land,
Who with his wealth and warriors embarks to cross the main,
An empire new to conquer for Heaven and for Spain.

'Twas on the isle of jewels they marshal well and long,
Then cross'd the narrow waters, six hundred warriors strong,
With steeds and lance and carbine, to conquer and to hold
The land of healing fountains, of glittering gems and gold;
And loud the thanks to Heaven, and tall the cross they rear.
('Twas then the way of nations, and were they not sincere?
Too oft we judge of others by light they never knew;
In ages past or coming perchance we'd change our view.)
Soon reared is stockade ample for those they leave behind,
Then with their steeds and banners through flowery vales they wind.
Thus forth a realm to conquer, and gold and glory gain,
Proud tread the knights of Portugal and cavaliers of Spain.

'Twas now no land of mountains, of terraced slopes and pines,
But sedgy bogs and cane-brakes, and thorny plants and vines.
Beneath the moaning cypress in mourning draped they find
No greeting friend before them, but lurking foe behind;

As thus for moons they wander through forest, fen, or
 glade,
By sedgy lakes and bayous they sorely are delayed,
Till Ortiz, long a captive unto a chieftain grand,
By him in kindness sent them, guides safely through the
 land
Unto the smiling hamlets of a people tall and brave,
Who prize a sturdy foeman, but scorn a cringing slave,
To homes of shelter welcome, 'mid golden fields of
 grain,
They greet the famished warriors, the cavaliers of Spain.

Long through the land they wander in search of gems
 and gold
In vain, and suffer hunger and sickness, thirst and cold;
Oft cheered by baseless legends, that lead them far
 astray,
In pathless rocky regions to wend their weary way,
Till from a craggy summit with joyful shout they gaze
Upon a land of hamlets and golden fields of maize.
A chieftain had each village, its temple and its priest,
And robes and signs and seasons for sacrifice and feast.
High in the level valley broad mounds of earth they
 raise
For lofty halls of chieftain, of council, or for praise,
And palisades encircle the hamlets of the plain,
When greeted by these pilgrims, the cavaliers of Spain.

In welcome through the valleys they eat and take their
 fill;
Resistless in the hamlets, they revel, rob, and kill;
And chieftain hold as hostage, to furnish slaves to bear
The burdens of the victors, relieved from toil and care,

Until from Tas-ta-lu-ca they cross Pi-u-che's stream,
And view within Mau-il-la the spears of warriors gleam.
In parley brief the chieftain, the hostage, and the slave,
Exchange the fetters galling for the weapons of the brave;
And then the slave and captor as sturdy warriors meet,
With battle-axe and sabre, all fight and none retreat.
But breast to breast, with blow and thrust, fast pile the heaps of slain,
The warriors' doom, in paint and plume, and belted knights of Spain.

Oh, hasten, bold Moscoso, charge fearless o'er the plain,
Ride down and thrust the foeman, and broader strew the slain.
From fallen steed De Soto remounts to quick restore
To ranks the warriors quenching their thirst 'mid pools of gore.
From *these* the shout of battle and bugle-blast prolong,
From *those* the clarion war-whoop and dying battle-song.
The shafts of stalwart warriors, fast as the mountain hail,
Crash through the shield and helmet, and pierce the coat of mail;
And feathered barbs are flying, like wintry flakes of snow,
And ghastly wounds are spouting, as geysers jet and flow.
Earth moans, as o'er her bosom fast flows the crimson tide
From wounds of countless peasants who round their altars died;
And 'neath the hoof of chargers, through trellised hills and dales,
Transpierced by lance and sabre, arise the dying wails,

When lo! from fiery torches, hurled 'mid the thatchy roofs,
A thousand red-tongued monsters career with blazing hoofs;
A lurid hell, they revel o'er maid and peasant slain,
And to it force the living, the mounted knights of Spain.

Grim sinks the king of splendor behind the field of flame;
Pale beams the queen of evening above the scene of shame;
Shrill rings the taunt defiant from warriors in the glade;
Chill grow the faint and dying, on gory couches laid.
No warming draught nor bandage, nor lint to stanch a wound;
None from the smouldering ruins will evermore be found.
Faint throbs the ebbing lifetide on weary comrade's breast;
Faint, fainter still and flickering, and two warriors are at rest.
Sad is the dirge and wailing, and muffled drum and fife,
'Neath banners draped and tattered, and pierced in bloody strife;
Reversed their swords and lances, and slow their measured tread,
As sadly on the morrow they bear the mangled dead.
Amid the holly shadows, upon the gory plain,
Uncoffined sleep and moulder two hundred sons of Spain.

Dim fades the gloomy vision, as wandering far and wide,
Through countless tramps and battles, to Mississippi's tide;
High o'er the waters rolling resistless to the main
They rear the cross as Christians, and claim the land for Spain;

Then o'er its turbid waters still onward far they roam
Through countless vales and hamlets, nor seek nor merit
    home,
Till in the craggy mountains these pilgrims, seeking gold,
Fade as the leaves of autumn from hunger, thirst, and
    cold;
Then southward, weary wandering through wintry wind
    and storm,
Till on the bold Arkansas they sleep in hamlets warm.
The prayers of peaceful owners for recompense were vain;
Naught had they left to give them, these wanderers from
    Spain.

Time, strife, and suffering dispel their golden dreams;
Homeward they turn in spring-time adown the swollen
    streams,
Until the Mississippi they shouting greet again,
Far down its turbid waters, anear the briny main;
But weary, wan, and sinking, and sadly needing those
Whose bones, alas! are bleaching along their trail of
    woes,
To build them barks of safety, yet haughty to the last,
Supplies demand of chieftain of maize and service vast.
No *cringing* menial answer, but haughty chief of braves,—
"Of *me*, the prince of warriors, claim food and toiling
    slaves;
And *you*, the heir of Heaven, the son of rolling sphere,
Dry up the mighty river, then come, you'll find me here.
If friend, I'll greet you grandly; if foe, no bended knee
Be stool for mounting charger; in life or death we're
    free."
A peer has met De Soto; another waiting stands;
It is remorse's fever and 'vengeful reeking hands,

Which from his couch of anguish, as galling captive
  chain,
Drag 'neath the turbid waters this cavalier of Spain.

Dim through the murky shadows I view Moscoso's band,
Far wandering through the deserts in search of golden
  land;
A remnant fierce and famished to Rio Grande* return,
One hamlet fill with plunder, and others wanton burn,
And harmless peasants chaining,—'tis not the land of
  those
Who strangers greet in friendship, or warriors meet as
  foes,—
To help in toil in forming a stockade broad and long,
And then brigantines seven, of plank and timbers strong;
And nails they forge of fetters torn from their dying
  slaves,
Or helmet, sword, or buckler of vanished comrade braves,
Then with the flood of waters launch boldly for the main,
This remnant of the warriors, these cavaliers of Spain.

Far comes the shout of triumph as breezes fill their sails;
Near swells the moans of dying and famished orphans'
  wails;
Faint falls the song of gladness from those we'll see no
  more;
Loud rings the clarion death-whoop of warriors seeking
  gore.
A hand is on my bosom, cold fingers clutch my hair,—
O God! it is a vision, and vanishes in air.

---

* As the Spaniards then called the Mississippi River

A steamer's screeching whistle, her shouting crew and
    bell,
Commingle with the tempest, unearthly din to swell;
Yet lingering from my vision awhile a phantom clings,
And from my ancient relics in fading cadence sings:
"Oh, freed we from our prison, our fetters, and our clay;
Where are our friends and comrades, and captors, where
    are they?
Where are the fields and camp-fires, the walls and pickets
    strong?
O'ergrown by mighty forests, sure we have slumbered
    long."
Yes, slumbered long and tranquilly, while friends and
    race are fled;
Another race has conquered, and mingles with your dead.
The tramp of mighty armies, the roar of bloody strife,
Of brother against brother, aroused you not to life.
As countless rills uniting a flood to swell the sea,
These brothers blend a nation, united, happy, free;
While plaintive moans the cypress, and dark the waters
    flow,
As in the days of Cortez, four hundred years ago,
Thus fades my midnight vision, thus ends my mournful
    strain,
Of the legend of De Soto, the cavalier of Spain.

NOTES.

THE CALUMET OF THE COTEAU.

¹ "Say, hast thou seen the cal-u-met of pink or purple bright,
A pipe-bowl in the council, a hatchet in the fight?"

The first white rovers of the seas who landed upon the shores of North America were uniformly met by armed, stalwart, red- or copper-colored warriors, led by some paint-and-plume-bedecked chieftain, who, with a spread robe or blanket and the curling azure smoke of the pipe of peace, welcomed them to their wild shore and rude hospitality.

This indeed seems to have ever been the custom in their intercourse with the whites and with each other. Be it a casual meeting upon the trail, a visit of friendship or business, a council for the adjustment of differences to avoid war, or for the ratification of the terms of peace, little is ever said, and positively nothing important done, until after the exchange of at least a few puffs of smoke from the never-wanting, forgotten, or neglected pipe of peace.

These are of various forms, but all having the orifice for the insertion of the stem at one end, extend to a capacious bowl or receptacle upon one side, usually at right angles therewith, for the indigenous tobacco, or, in its absence, Kin-no-ke-nick osier-bark, or other fragrant inflammable substances. For use upon ordinary occasions they were made of a great variety of rocky substances, and, together with the stem, were ornamented according to the caprice or circumstances of the maker or subsequent owner. This class of pipes are articles of sale, barter, valued tokens of esteem, as presents to friends in life, and, less frequently, as bequests at death; as, from the nearly universal belief of the North American Indians that all things animate and inanimate alike possess souls, these pipes, a supply of tobacco and food, as well as his weapons, utensils, ornaments, apparel, and blankets, occasionally his war horse, and sometimes his widow, or widows, are buried with the warrior gone, so that in the happy hunting-grounds beyond the mountains he may there renew life, its pursuits and its pleasures, as he left it here.

But in the grand councils, for the adjustment of disputes of boundaries, formation of alliances, or the ratification of the terms of peace among nations, the indispensable ceremonial pipe of peace is the yellow-mottled, pink, or purple calumet from the sacred quarry of the legendary fossilized flesh of the antediluvian progenitors of the race of red men, usually bearing the totem of the owner, clan, or tribe, or all of them, and which were never regular articles of barter or sale, and seldom of transfer, save in compacts of alliance or confederation of tribes or nations, when they were exchangeable. Hence its transfer to other races was sacrilegious; and of the countless pipes peacefully obtained of the Indians by the early white men, it is believed that few, if any, were genuine sacred calumets; and the location, even approximately, of the sacred quarry, or, as figuratively called, mountain, was for a long time unknown to white men.

Tradition relates that the first devout Frenchmen who visited the falls of the Father of Waters in 1680 were greeted by the appearance of St. Anthony, the patron saint of the expedition, who, from amid the spray above the falls, warned them that a great council of the nations of red men had recently ordained that no pale-face should be allowed to nearer approach the sacred calumet quarry; and, also, that he was rewarded for his fidelity and the event commemorated by their attaching his name to the falls, which they still retain.

These well-known falls are 380 miles by direct railroad connection, and fully twice that distance by the ancient route of nations up the St. Peter's—now Minnesota—River and coteau route, from the sacred quarry, which, although in the land of the Dakotas, is some miles east of the border of that Territory, in Pipestone County, Minnesota, as now organized.

It is situated near the southern end of the great "Coteau des Prairies" of the old French voyageurs, and upon the small calumet affluent of the Big Sioux River, which is now called the Pipestone Creek, near the drainage divide of the Mississippi and Missouri Rivers. From the summit of this coteau divide the long parallel swells uniform in character, but charmingly diversified in outline, stretch, like the waves of a fossilized ocean, away, away, until the verdure of earth and the azure of heaven blend in the cloudless horizon of one of the most charming rural landscapes of earth, even still while being spanned by the iron rail and dotted by the dwellings, the grain-fields, verdant groves, and thriving villages of the all-progressive race of destiny, over the rude tumuli, mouldering bones, and crumbling land-marks of the wandering race fast fading away.

That the unique surface conformation of this region results from enormous groovings and deposits during the glacial period and countless ages of subsequent erosion is fully proven by the surface and character of the soil, the countless huge erratic blocks, or lost boulders strewn broadcast upon it, as the sacred eggs of the genii in the Little Calumet or Pipestone Valley, the countless deep parallel groovings upon all the exposed rocks of the cliffs as well as the valley, and the evident abrading effects upon them of the frosts and the infrequent but severe storms of a high latitude and a moderately elevated, open, and windy region.

The operation of some or all of these agencies has produced a valley two miles in length, extending somewhat east of north and west of south from the midway and deepest portion of the falls on the Calumet or Pipestone Creek, where over thirty feet of the horizontally-banded and cross-sectioned, vitreous, beautiful flesh- or pink-colored stone rises in nearly vertical but broken-edged walls.

The creek is barely a permanent stream save in spring-time or floods, when it is a prairie deluge, breaking over the ragged cliffs in several additional cascades; but the four pools or lakelets along the stream within a mile northwesterly are all rocky and permanent, well stocked with pickerel and other fish, and often literally covered with ducks, geese, and other water-fowl.

The carpet of herbage and flowers along this creek and chain of lakelets must have ever been a chosen haunt of buffalo, elk, deer, and antelope; and a view from the sacrificial altar upon the cliff-borders of this sacred vale of refuge, and the pilgrims from countless nations, engaged in bathing, in peaceful amusements, or in quarrying the sacred pipestone, must have ever been one of the most unique and interesting ever witnessed by man in any age or clime.

The sacred quarry is about one-third of a mile west from the cliffs and parallel with them, and whether or not its discovery really resulted from the pilgrims trailing the white or medicine bison or buffalo through the creek, as related in the legend, it is evident it was first opened along the creek and north of it, the more recent as well as extensive excavations extending south of it to a point opposite the legendary abode of the genii.

The real vein of mottled purple pipestone is a horizontally-bedded and stratified steatite rock aggregating eighteen or twenty inches in thickness, of which only two or three of the bottom strata are thick enough for the sacred calumet,—and this during much of the year is beneath the water,—the material upon its first removal being soft and easily carved and polished in any desired form, which it ever retains, somewhat hardening and deepening in color with age.

As this pipestone is beneath two or three feet of soil and six or eight of vitreous rocks, only the peculiar fracture of the latter into angular blocks of from four to six feet in length and half as wide and thick could have enabled a rude people destitute of good tools or mechanical appliances to make excavations fully a mile in length and from fifty to two hundred feet in width,—remains which must ever be viewed as one of the marvellous exhibitions of the persistence of man in securing an ornament or sustaining a superstition.

2 " But the bison, so lofty, so fleet, and so white,
Oh! mar not his beauty, but follow his flight!"

The white, or medicine, curly bison of the parks, or the shaggy buffalo of the plains.

They are extremely rare, and, like the medicine wolf, wolverine, and other white individual animals of dark-colored species, are perhaps albinos, and certainly ever objects of mysterious awe, and usually of ceremonious sacrifice, and hence in this case symbolic.

3 " These five eggs I leave for your witness and mine."

These famous eggs of the legendary monster eagle are really that number of huge drift granite boulders from some distant unknown source, and each from ten to thirty feet in diameter.

They are found in a line against each other, fronting the Calumet Creek from the south, about midway in the little valley, extending from the cliffs of the sacred quarry of fossilized warriors, rising thirty or forty feet above, to the modern quarry, six feet beneath its grassy but angular rock-strewn surface.

<blockquote>⁴ " Lo ! neath are two grottos for Wa-root-ka's home."</blockquote>

These Wa-root-kas are the two legendary female genii or local goddesses of the sacred quarry, who, in two little grottos between these eggs, are ever alternately slumbering and watching the sacred quarry.

These rocks, and more notably flat-surfaced rocks about them, are nearly covered by the carved or painted totems of the countless pilgrims who have, during untold ages, sacrificed to these guardians of the quarry for the privilege of removing fragments therefrom.

<blockquote>⁵ " Bold Chey-enne and Da-ko-ta, the latter called Si-oux."</blockquote>

Da-ko-ta is the Indian name for the confederacy of tribes by the whites called Si-oux.

This latter name is of somewhat doubtful origin, by some believed to be derived from the Algonquin name Nad-a-was-see-wak, or the people who are shake-like, from the proverbial sly, crafty character of these people. By others the name is deemed the corruption of a pigeon French word little less complimentary. But of the name of this people in the sign language there is no question, which is given by drawing the edge of the open right hand from left to right across the throat, literally "cut-throat;" nor do these names belie their character or their legendary origin as the progeny of the ferocious War-Eagle and the sneaking but ever-famished and voracious Cayouta, or Prairie-Wolf.

This name is properly expressed in two closely-connected, quickly-spoken syllables, as used in this work, as if spelled Si-ou, although the whites now usually pronounce it as if spelled Soo, in one syllable.

<blockquote>⁶ " In jasper cairn they buried the maid and warrior gone,
And bright their totems painted upon the walls of stone."</blockquote>

This cairn mode of burial is and probably ever has been practised at this sacred calumet quarry, although extremely unusual with the Indians of the great plains and coteaus, few of whom are elsewhere ever buried in the earth or cairns, but usually encased, with their weapons and implements, in blankets and green buffalo-hide, are placed by their friends upon inaccessible ledges of rocks, in forked trees, or, in the absence of both of these, upon scaffolds for the pappoose, squaw, or dog-soldier, or in gorgeous teepee for the chieftain gone. But the belief that both the cliff and quarry of the pipestone are the sacred relics of the antediluvian (in part) progenitors of their race seems to have ever prompted them to endure every privation and danger in pilgrimages from distant nations, to secure not only unpolluted fragments of the sacred pipestone, but, in case of their dying at the Mecca of their hopes and journeying, to also secure a burial-cairn of the abundant and wide-spread fragments of the cliff.

The countless numbers of these cairns in the valley, upon the cliff, and for miles upon the surrounding coteau, literally form a sacred cemetery in a land of savages; and as these purple- or flesh-colored rocks are seemingly glazed too hard for carving with any tool known to these people, many of them and portions of the cliff are nearly covered with the fading painted totems of the pilgrims who have mouldered to dust beneath them.

7 "The woolly-sheep and big-horn."

The two distinct and extremely dissimilar varieties of the wild sheep of the Rocky Mountain region.

The famous big-horn, thus named from the enormous symmetrical horns of the adult males, is the taller, more active, darker-haired, and more beautiful animal, and is also far the most numerous and best known.

While the big-horn has much the appearance of a black-tail deer, with the head and enormous horns of a domestic ram, the white sheep with his curly under and long shaggy outer coating of hair, with his small, sharp, backward turned and beautiful black horns, much resembles a huge goat, only he is web-footed for travelling on the snow fields of the most elevated regions, such as those of the main Rocky Mountains around the Deer Lodge, Big-Hole, and Bitter-Root Valleys, from which he never ventures far or long remains.

8 "Bestride fleet hornless bison."

This appellation for a horse, eagle's wings for the sails of the schooner, or big canoe, long-knife for sword, bosom-totem for the buckle-plate of the cross-belt, war-bonnet for the helmet-cap, the flashing lightning, startling thunder, and deadly barbless arrows, are in accordance with the well-known Indian characteristic of naming objects to them new or mysterious.

9 " Then from the ' Mighty Medicine' in terror fled amazed."

Literally, the great mysterious unknown; for medicine in Indian does not signify medicinal preparations to cure disease by their inherent properties, but rather anything mysterious, awe-inspiring, or fearful, including the abominable paints and poisonous decoctions of their medicine-men, who are not skilful physicians, but crafty, conjuring magicians.

10 " Pure Hen-ne-pin and Du-luth visit for good the shore."

These daring explorers, like Marquette and most of the early French rovers of the great Northwestern lakes and plains, were zealous and devout missionaries of the cross, than whom few men in any age have left a more brilliant record of combined heroic daring and Christian purity, fortitude, and forbearance, and who should in no sense be confounded with the crafty, rum-selling, laws-of-God-and-man-defying fur-traders who followed them.

11 " Till the prairie Min-ne-tan-ka."

Or, in the Dakota language, Min-ne, water; Tanka, great, or, as necessarily reversed in English, is literally Great water; but, when properly understood and arranged, signifies the Great River of the Prairies,—*i.e.*, the Mississippi.

12 " With purple pipe the chieftain first heavenward points above."

With a thorough knowledge and heartfelt desire, I confess my utter inability to properly portray the matchless deliberation, solemnity, and awe of the invocation of Heaven to witness the sincerity and punish the treachery of those who, with a deliberate puff of the sacred calumet pipe of peace, in council pledge

"Each as a friend to know,
While sun and moon shall circle, or crystal waters flow."

13 " Naught care they for the sufferings, the hunger, thirst, or cold
Of agonizing victims, so with gore they gather gold."

Alas! now, as it ever has been, too lamentably and undeniably true, beside the sanctuaries of the Sabbath in a Christian land, as well as in the trader's lair among the filthy wigwams of the painted savage, wherever rum is sold.

14 "For wife to grace the harem, and firm unite his race."

"Wife," often a temporary mistress to the trader in his harem, which far too many trading-posts are cursed with, and ever have been, and thus, and from the roving habits of all parties, less a permanent home of any semblance of virtue, than a noisy haunt of profit-seeking alliance and alluring, transient vice.

15 "Tower high o'er crystal waters huge crags of crumbling slate."

The Maiden's Rock, or Leap, on the eastern shore of Lake Pepin, famous in Indian legends from the death of Min-ne-ha-ha and her chieftain lover, Min-ne-o-la, as herein related.

If the tourist should find this cliff more of a crumbling sandstone than a slate, he may safely charge the error to poetical license for the purpose of symphony in the rhyme.

16 "Then thrust aside degraded, to delve in kennel vile!"

"Kennel vile!" Trading-posts are notorious haunts of dogs, mainly mongrels of not only every domestic variety, but also crosses with the fox, cayouta, and sometimes the ferocious buffalo-wolf of the plains, together with their attendant venom and vermin.

17 "The secret passage opens."

The early trading-posts were usually constructed upon the dry, sandy, or gravelly bluffs to lakes or rivers, for the purpose of setting the stockade pickets, and for the construction of secret passage-ways to the hidden powder-magazine and caches for valuable goods, as well as for the purpose of retreat, or securing reinforcements, or secrecy of their dusky amours; and in this case (presumably through the connivance of some friend) known to the females, but not to the War-Eagle.

18 "Still oft in wave-kissed grottos sing they at 'Maiden's Leap.'"

With these wave-kissed grottos is always connected some tradition of love or slaughter, and frequently of both; and the moaning echoes of the receding ripples in the hidden chambers are ever attributed to the wailing dirge of the fallen heroes or heroines of the legend, and hence are ever places of unrivalled interest in both fact and fiction.

> [19] " And thou, Mis-sis-sip-pi, bear'st temples in gladness,
> With loud strains of music their progress to trace."

It seems scarcely necessary to state that these stanzas refer to the magnificent three-decked steam-packets and their cliff-echoing calliopes upon the Mississippi and other mighty western rivers.

> [20] " Bury purple cal'met peaceful;
> Quench its azure smoke;
> Grasp the hatchet crimson reeking,
> Death at every stroke."

As burying the hatchet is the ceremonial manner as well as the figurative mode of expressing the ratification of a treaty of peace, even thus was burying the calumet pipe, with its azure smoke and peaceful memories, the appropriate expression of the wine- and stepmother-frenzied War-Eagle in opening a war of merciless extermination upon his own offspring by an ever-peaceful and affectionate former consort.

> [21] "Thus soon the Wa-kan-she-cha had crushed or slain the race."

Wa-kan, mysterious; she-cha, bad; or bad mysterious one, or devil she-devil, which the entire history of this cayouta wife of War-Eagle proves her to have truly been.

> [22] " And 'mid the wild roses with carnage once red."

Few scenes upon the border are more pleasing than the profusion, variety, and fragrance of the wild roses; and from the large brightred, orange, or yellow-tinted seed-balls, which, under the name of rosebuds, hang upon the bushes all winter as food for birds, and in dire necessity for men, the numerous streams and valleys derive their names.

A humble but hardy variety of the rose thrives and blooms amid the cactus of such sterile coteau plains as those of the Custer slaughterfield, and are there actually found.

> [23] "On the crest of the coteau."

Where the gallant Custer and the last of his band went down as a phalanx, and where, with due deference to the views of others, in my humble judgment, they should have ever remained. It is the abrupt terminus of the long coteau-ridge upon which they, retreating fighting, fell, sloping somewhat in all directions, steeply but beautifully upon three of them,. thus commanding a clear view of the entire Indian village and valley of the Little Big-Horn (or Custer River) for many miles, with all the slaughter-fields of that day, save those of Reno's, the first of which is somewhat hidden by timber, and the last completely by an intervening bluff.

Some of these words were inspired and written upon meeting the returning train and the remainder of them upon that consecrated crest, the day following the removal of all found of the officers' remains.

I *still* cherish the opinion, *then* formed, that few places earthly are as lovely, and none so fitting for a warrior's cairn or hero's monument, as where some of them fell; and all should have been gathered, and, beneath a fitting monument, allowed undisturbed repose until Gabriel's reveille should rouse them to their last rally.

> 24 " Nor bold as men of courage 'gainst remnant on the hill,
> But prowling 'long the border, the innocent to kill."

The failure of the congregated hostile savages of the Sioux and several other Indian nations to follow up the rebuff of Crook, the slaughter of Custer, and defeat of Reno by the speedy extermination of the remnant of the regiment upon the hill, and then cutting up the troops of Terry and Gibbons in detail, as they, by the concerted action of organized troop, could have done, but instead, as they really did, by revelling in brutal mutilation of the dead upon the field, until surprised and stampeded from it by the handful of troops under Terry, and then breaking up into recruiting-parties or scalping-bands along the distant border, they clearly exemplified the true Indian character and management in nearly all their wars with the whites.

> 25 " From the fairy Min-ne-ha-ha and lover's wailing strand."

Lover's wailing strand of Lake Pepin, as noted in the stanzas of this legend.

> "Swells one loud wail of agony from sea of flame and gore,
> Like scream of dying eagle, then silence evermore!"

For the credit of humanity this fate has not befallen the main portion of the Sioux nation, although it seemed impending, if not, indeed, just and inevitable, at the time when the words were written upon the steamer "Ashland," while ascending the Yellowstone River with General Miles, soon after his Rose-Bud fight of 1877.

> 26 "On the banners of this people let his pinions soar above,
> With my maiden's cap of Justice, of Liberty, and Love!"

Pure, loving, and faithful was the character, heroic the life, and tragic the death of the Laughing Water, Min-ne-ha-ha, and immortal her dirge, as with the blended voice of her, in life and in death, ever-faithful lover, Min-ne-o-la, it re-echoes along the cliffs, or in mournful fading cadence vanishes 'mid the whispering ripples in the wave-kissed grottos of Lake Pepin's tranquil shore.

Still it is not she, but her heroic mother, the remnant of the primeval, and parent of the best of the modern red men, who was the heroine of this legend.

Whether in the eagle's nest upon the cliff as the confiding refugee of a drowning race, a willing listener to the complaints and ameliorator of the wants and woes of her people as a queen, or as a faithful, forgiving wife and loving mother, indeed, everywhere in her entire legendary history are harmoniously blended all the virtues and none of the vices or failings of the real or legendary heroines of other races and climes.

Although her heroic efforts to save her daughter Min-ne-ha-ha are requited by the speedy death of herself and subsequent relentless persecution by her rum-frenzied and Cayouta-second-wife-instigated War-Eagle, still her pure, confiding spirit ever hovers in love over the dwindling remnant of her race, and in the hour of just retribution upon that of her fiendish successor in the love and favor of her debased husband, still she manifests towards his memory, in all their purity, those unselfish, forgiving attributes of the female character which in every age and clime have been its greatest and most mysterious charm.

All her cruel and countless wrongs are overlooked or forgotten, and from the ethereal vault of heaven she only recalls the memory of War Eagle as the chivalric rescuer and loving husband of her youth, and father of her offspring; and in *his* hour of humiliation and despair, and of *her* triumph, as the herald of heaven to affix upon the banner of the victorious race of progress the deluge-spared emblems of her primeval race, her " maiden's cap of Justice, of Liberty, and

Love," she, with smiling angels' gliding grace, plants beneath it the long-retained and cherished plumes and pinion quills plucked from those of her War-Eagle chieftain in the days of his purity and pride.

And thus, as related in this legend, was it ordained that the emblems upon the azure field of the battle-flag of the nation of the nations of earth, the chosen land of refuge for the down-trodden and oppressed images of God from every clime and race, should not be debasing imitations of the tyranny and crime-stained banners of other lands, but rather the rescued indigenous emblems of the primeval, the piercing lance and arrow of the warrior red men, and the heavenward-soaring pinions of the fearless battle-eagle of our own!

[27] THE GOBLIN-LAND.

This wild, chaotic region of eroded lava, within or adjoining the northeastern portion of the National Park, was named the Hoodoo, or Goblin-Land, in 1870 by the first party of white men who are known to have ever visited it.

Some members of the party were there killed by the Indians; and, accompanied by one of the survivors, I was driven back by them in 1878, but succeeded in the exploration of much of it in 1880, a brief narrative of which, together with illustrations of some of the goblin forms, may be found on pages 6-9 of my report of that year.

Reference to these regions may also be found on page 47, and in the map accompanying my report of 1881.

In this poetical legend I have sought to blend the traditions and heathen mythology of the sheep-eater aborigines of these regions with the teachings of Inspiration and the records of geology regarding the horizontal columns of the huge vertical dykes, fantastic pillars, façades, and domes, the crumbling archways, the tortuous labyrinths and monster goblin-forms of this marvellous extension of the famous Wonder-Land.

> [28] "The black eagle soars round the pinnacle high
> Till a wild lamb perceiving, as a bolt from the sky,
> In his talons quick bears him for a feast in the glade,
> Near the lion low crouching, whose dinner is made
> Of victor and victim, in tanglewood shade."

This is a correct statement of what I once saw in the Goblin Labyrinths, where the great black eagles in vast numbers appear to subsist mainly upon the carcasses of the wild lambs which they carry, or of the sheep which in rapid noisy circling they first bewilder, and then with wing or talon, or both, assist in hurling from the tottering crests or crags to the jagged rocks hundreds of feet below.

The feasts of these crafty eagles upon such carcasses are sometimes terminated by those of the couchant cougar, or mountain-lion, or of the sneaking wolverine upon their own.

[20] "Then man, hairy giant, strode forth in his might."

This stanza is believed to express in a concise and connected manner the attributes of the biped man, the possessor of an immortal soul, as distinct from the quadruped or other animals destitute thereof, which are,—

First. "Erect like his Maker," which, unlike any other known animal, is his natural and habitual position in locomotion.

Second. "With knowledge of right."

Reflection, reasoning, the faculty of tracing effect to cause and cause to effect, and ability, possessed by no other animal, of imparting connectedly to others or of transmitting to posterity the results of his experience in life.

"Third. "Inventor of weapons."

All other animals rely upon brute force, speed, or cunning.

Man alone invents, manufactures, or habitually uses weapons in his combats, or tools or implements in his other avocations; and these he is ever improving, while the products of instinct are ever the same. The comb of the first wasp or honey-bee, the nest of the original oriole bird, and the brush-dam and wickeup of the whisker-faced, paddle-tailed progenitors of the beaver-dam builders of earth were as marvellous evidences of skill and of adaptability for the desired purposes as are those of to-day or as they ever will be.

Fourth. "First builder of fire."

Other animals may, as they will, bask in the rays of the sun, or beside a hot spring, and sometimes warm themselves by a fire already kindled, but only man ever produces, preserves, or materially utilizes one.

"Fifth. "Lone trader of trophies."

Other animals may unite to slaughter, but seldom peaceably divide, and never exchange, the fragments obtained, or, as has been well said, "No dog trades his bone;" nor does any other animal than man barter what he has for what he desires, or ever use a medium of exchange therefor.

Sixth. "With soul to soar higher."

Despite the able efforts of some men of pre-eminent ability of the present and the past to refute the doctrine of an immortal soul to temporarily people a human tenement of clay, and permanently inhabit some unknown realm of weal or woe, still the theory in some form is and ever has been wellnigh co-extensive with the human race. This is notable with the leading tribes of the North American Indians, whose paradise is some enchanting island or lovely park, and their perdition a chilling alkali desert, or some fire-hole basin of seething poisonous gases beyond the scorchy deserts or snowy mountains of the earth on which we dwell.

> [30] "Men, mermaids, and monsters, each sphinx-like in place,
> And mountains hurled o'er them, from Heaven hides trace."

As, to this date, less than a score of white men, none of whom were professional scientists, have visited the Goblin Labyrinths, their relative position and rank among the marvels of this wonderful region is yet to be accorded.

But to the mountaineers who have visited them it requires little superstitious conjuring to imagine that the huge goblin forms which our daring mountain-horses instinctively shun are the men, monsters, and reptiles of a degenerate and licentious world, overwhelmed, hidden, and fossilized by enormous overflows of lava, mud, and slime, and unearthed by the grooving, furrowing, and tunnelling of countless ages of sub-alpine erosion.

> [31] "And men of the mountains, of Sheep-Eater band,
> Of game and of plunder make sacrifice grand
> To monster stone-gods in the weird 'Goblin-Land.'"

The maps accompanying my reports of 1880 and of 1881 show the position of the most eligible site and evidently ever-favorite camping-place for the aborigines of these regions, and where there are now the remains of forty-two lodges, some of which are still standing.

Upon my visit of 1880 this camp was strewn with the torn and faded remnants of male and female apparel, household goods, and utensils, some of which were brought away as mournful mementos of bloody raids upon the distant border, from which, and from a knowledge of the superstitious customs and habits of these people, rather than from direct evidence in this case, I venture the language of burnt-offering in the poem to these weird monsters of stone, which to them must have ever been objects of mysterious awe, and hence of sacrifice.

MYSTIC LAKE OF WONDER-LAND.

[32] "And chilling blasts resistless come
Adown thy fingers, palm, and thumb."

The early rovers and their maps of these regions represented the unique contour of the Yellowstone Lake as more nearly resembling an open human hand than subsequent explorations seem to justify.

Still, its resemblance to the extended palm of the right hand, with the Upper Yellowstone entering the extremity of the little finger from the south, the main river discharging from the wrist at the north, the forefinger now severed from Delusion Lake, the second finger much shortened, with the western thumb relatively enlarged, and the main lake or palm nearly as wide as it is long, which is more striking from some adjacent snowy peaks than upon a map, is so evident that these names of the various portions of the lake will doubtless long adhere to them.

[33] "No tent can stand, no blanket save
From biting blasts that round us rave."

Literally true, and mainly written when beached and frozen-in near the mouth of Explorer's Creek, as briefly noted on page 11 of my official report of 1880.

[34] "Yet practice crimes that dark disgrace
Our Christian creed and bearded race."

Alas! too often and too undeniably true.

With relatively few worthy exceptions, the policy of white men has ever been to wantonly crush, or to employ alike the worthy and the unworthy red men as allies to assail and divide them, to practise and condone crimes, pension outlaws, and grant annuities to the bloodiest bands of savages, in order to secure treaties ceding lands.

Meanwhile the steadfast adherence to peaceful possession of valuable agricultural, timbered, or mineral lands by their unquestioned Indian owners is deemed the sole unpardonable crime of the race, only condoned by the surrender of the land or their lives, and often of both, after unchronicled acts of heroism, rivalling those of the lauded patriots of our own or of other lands.

<blockquote>35 "Vases and urns from nature's hand."</blockquote>

The prolongation of Mary's Bay, near the Indian Pond, between the mouth of Pelican Creek and Steamboat Point, upon the Yellowstone Lake, was by myself named Concretion Cove, from the countless numbers and various forms of concretions which there fairly shingle the wave-lashed beach.

On pages 15-17 of my report of 1880 may be found a description of this location and these concretions, together with a theory as to their formation; and on pages 70 and 71 of that of 1881 illustrations of some of these unique forms.

<blockquote>36 "And finny forms beneath the wave
For angler's bait hot current brave,
To find, alas! like human fool,
A barb concealed and seething pool."</blockquote>

Of the countless marvels of the National Park, few have been more ridiculed, and the reality of none is now better established, than that the large and beautiful but worm-infested trout of the Yellowstone Lake at several localities, notably where our trail leaves the end of the thumb for the Shoshone Lake, may be caught in countless numbers in the lake and cooked in hissing pools without the angler changing his position or removing them from the hook.

<blockquote>37 "And thence from nauseous hissing rill
Sweet flow'ry vale with poisons fill."</blockquote>

This description of the changing character of many of the rivulets in the Wonder-Land may be verified by any tourist who will follow them from their snow or crystal spring fountains through nauseous ponds or basins of hissing, sulphurous pools, and the flowery grove-dotted vale below them, all perhaps within the distance of a mile or two.

A typical case is the crystal rill from the snows of Mount Chittenden, upon which I have often camped above Turbid Lake, upon the shores of which, upon its southeastern tributary, or along its outlet, no human being would wish to camp, or could long endure the sulphur fumes and poisonous gases of an earthly purgatory.

> [88] "And islands thine, rock-ribbed and high,
> With snowy crests amid the sky:
> Inverted, mirrored 'neath the waves,
> Seem isles to greet 'mid islands' graves."

While Stevenson's, Frank's, and some of the smaller islands of the Yellowstone Lake are sandy, and but slightly elevated above its surface, several of the headlands and long promontories, as that between the third and little finger, are bold, craggy, and basaltic peaks, having only relatively low, narrow connections with the mainland. These, in the usually deep tranquil blue waters at their base, are often reflected so accurately as to reproduce them inverted beneath the waves, as here described.

> [89] "For food their flesh, for hunting-shirt,
> Their vacant coat with belt begirt?"

From necessity, convenience, or utility, the Indians, half-breeds, and often the white rovers of the border, use robes, overcoats, boots, and caps of the hides of the wolf, wolverine, bear, or buffalo, dressed with the fur on, and hunting-shirts, leggins, and moccasins of elk-, sheep-, or deer-skins dressed without it.

In fact, the only cloth fabric which I have ever found a reliable protection alike from the merciless storms, the thorn, and weather-worn points of the shrubs and branches of those mountain regions, was the famous Hudson Bay mountain-coat.

This, with a half-cape, was made of cloth having a warp nearly as coarse and strong as fish-lines, and woof of twisted beaver or other fur with a very heavy nap, and, although common in those regions forty or fifty years ago, has for a long time been unobtainable.

Like these garments, the flint-lock gun and bull-boat of the past, the days of the hunting-shirt, the moccasin, and even the buffalo and his robe, are rapidly passing away; and hence these quoted and succeeding stanzas are, it is hoped, pardonable from one who has participated in two eras of border-life, and has ever earnestly sought to assist in hastening a better one for those who are soon to follow.

GALLANT CHARLEY REYNOLDS.

> ⁴⁰ "Once the chosen scout of Stanley,
> Often Ludlow's mountain guide,
> Then with me erst true and manly,—
> Thou who with our Custer died!"

Few of the daring scouts of the border ever acquired a greater number of friends, a more brilliant record, or met a more tragic or lamented fate than the gallant Charley Reynolds.

Upon our return from the National Park late in 1875, he remained at Fort Lincoln, where he was employed as chief of scouts, and as such led them in the Custer campaign until, with Bloody Knife and others, he was cut off from Reno's left flank in his hasty retreat from the ambuscade in the fated valley of the Little Big-horn on the day of the Custer massacre, and there fell bravely fighting until nearly covered by fallen steeds and foes.

From the half-breed French scout, T. T. Gerhard, who witnessed and, by concealment in the willows, alone escaped the massacre of those thus cut off, I learned the location, and after the removal of the bones of Custer and other officers in 1877, found and removed those of Reynolds, together with all of his well-known beautiful golden hair, which savage ghoul and famished wolf had spared. Some of this I still retain, but the most of it has been scattered far and wide, notably in Kentucky, in the earnest but fruitless effort to find his birthplace or his kindred and heirs; nor have I ever learned much of his history in addition to that published with this poem in my journal of "Rambles in the Far West" soon after his death, from which I quote as follows:

"After the removal of the officers' remains, the scout Baronet and myself remained upon or near the field until driven from it by Indian scouts, as may be found in a note to 'Reynolds's Dirge,' a portion of which was then written.

"As stated, we were much together in the Bad Lands, and nearly constantly upon the steamboat, and our excursions from it while descending the Missouri to Fort Lincoln, where we parted.

"He was engaged as chief of scouts for this campaign, hoping for its successful close in time for him and other mountain friends to accompany me to the Centennial, and, returning, spend the coming winter at my suburban home. He was perhaps thirty years of age, light complexion and hair, of medium height, but compact build, moral, temperate, mild, and quiet, until emergency called forth the matchless nerve and daring that made him the leading shot and scout of the Missouri or the Yellowstone. He was frank but not confiding. I never heard his nativity, and though his expressed desire to see an eastern city, and much of his appearance indicated a born mountaineer, still his morals, his quiet, refined manners, and a pervading melancholy when alone or at leisure, alike suggested a better rearing and a crushing misfortune or thrilling tragedy somewhere along his brief but checkered pathway. Premeditated crime I cannot believe of 'Lonesome Charley,' as he was often called; but scions of many wealthy families, especially from the Southern border States, during the closing scenes of the Rebellion, sought amid the mines and the mountains of the West a refuge from harrowing memories of ravaged homes and slaughtered friends; and several trifling incidents lead me to suspect that he was one of them.

" 'Mid shadows of the setting sun, echoes from the evening gun at Fort Buford roused us from hours of pensive wanderings 'mid the ruins of old Fort Union and the cemetery near Fort Buford, when, with a last lingering look at the turfy tomb of slaughtered friends, and with a heart too full for utterance, I was leaving the enclosure in silence, when Charley, in quiet but frank, earnest manner, said, ' Comrade, I am dreaming where a year hence will find us.' Prophetic dread, my noble fated comrade! That was at eve of September 25, 1875. Upon the eve of June 25 following, his scalped and mutilated body lay amid and nearly covered by foes, slaughtered by his avenging hand at the crimson ford of the Little Horn. July 25 my last letter to him was returned, soiled and worn, but unopened. September 25, by a protecting Providence kept at my peaceful home, sorrowfully I spent the closing eve of the fated year in penning the following poetry in feeling, if not in fact, sacred to the memory of that comrade of a year ago, far, far away."

It seems proper to here state that the foregoing poem and note were written before personally visiting the battle-field and finding that Reynolds was killed in or beside the "Crimson Ford," as from the first publication was then supposed.

[41] PILGRIMS OF THE YELLOWSTONE.

This legend is less a narrative of the sufferings and fate of any one party than a portrayal of the dangers, privations, and sufferings of all, and the slaughter of, alas! too many of the gold-seeking pilgrims who, under Bridger, Bozeman, and other daring pathfinders, literally left a trail of gore from the Platte to the Yellowstone in fighting their way to found an empire in the Gallatin and other lovely valleys of Montana prior to and during the ferocious Red Cloud Sioux war.

THE CAPTIVE MAIDEN.

[42] "Rise, my muse, sing of a maiden
Captive on the coteau wild."

This poem was written by request of the lamented Major Meacham, and was mainly published in his *Council Fire*.

It is deemed an essentially correct narrative of the valor of the chieftain lover, and heroic death of the captive maiden after the Rose-Bud fight of General Miles with the Cheyennes in 1877.

THE WONDER-LAND.

[43] "Oh, for wisdom in the councils
Of our nation great,
To protect these matchless wonders
From a ruthless fate!"

This poem was written in Washington, and used in manuscript in the spring of 1878 to aid in securing the first appropriation of funds ever made by Congress to protect, preserve, and improve the people's heritage of wonders in the Yellowstone National Park, and hence the language of the last verse, as above quoted.

BOLD HERO OF THE BORDER.

" "In lair of hidden gulches, in Woody Mountain wilds."

Woody Mountain is a timbered outlier of the Little Rocky Mountains, between the Missouri River at the mouth of the Musselshell and the British possessions, and from its abundance of fuel, water, yawning gulches, and wash-outs coulees, an admirable position for defensive warfare.

As such it was chosen by Chief Joseph, after having defeated or outgeneralled and distanced all known pursuers, and losing the most of his enormous herd of horses by the treachery of his old allies, the ever-crafty Crows.

It was this which prevented, if he desired, his reaching Sitting Bull, over the British border, before the flanking arrival of General Miles. Chief Joseph's camps throughout the National Park and the adjacent regions were uniformly well chosen and rudely but craftily prepared for defence; and his crossing mighty rivers, scaling snowy mountains, and traversing yawning cañons in a continuous migration of his whole people for a distance of nearly two thousand miles, mainly through the wildest, most elevated, craggy, least known, and least accessible portion of the United States, without forage, commissary, medicines, or supplies other than furnished by nature or captured from his cordon of able foes, must, all things considered, stand unrivalled in the history of border warfare upon this continent.

That Chief Joseph viewed with derision Generals Howard, Gibbon, Sturgis, and others, really worthy officers, whom he had defeated or distanced, is well known; that he was ignorant of the flank movement of General Miles is evident; and that he relied upon Sitting Bull for aid in defence of his camp and immense booty captured on the Missouri, and the slaughter of his pursuers if they ventured to assail his chosen position, seems very probable; and hence only the terrible onslaught of General Miles's unexpected forces in a terrific snow-storm, the death of Looking-Glass, his ablest chief, the utter failure of aid from Sitting Bull, and the approach of Howard and other pursuers, resulted in his capture when nearly in sight of the British line.

⁴⁵ " Then came the parley herald,—no servile cringing foe,
But chieftain with his rifle, the victors' terms to know."

In this way only, dauntless to the last, would Chief Joseph sue for terms of surrender, and even then accept such only as seem to have reflected more credit upon the valor of the Nez-Perces in the conditions named than the reputed failure of their proper fulfilment did upon the civil representatives of the government.

STALWART YEOMAN.

⁴⁶ " Not from hall of the Washburns,
Who so long have honor'd Maine,
But lowly ' Buckeye' cabin
Our stalwart yeoman came."

General H. D. Washburn was born and reared a hunter in the then wilds of Northwestern Ohio. I there first knew him, an active, ambitious youth; thence a surveyor in Western Indiana; from there he became an active soldier during the Rebellion, returning a brigadier-general, to be at once elected to Congress over the great Democratic champion, Daniel Voorhees, often called the " Tall Sycamore of the Wabash."

Upon my arrival from the Upper Yellowstone in June, 1870, I found him surveyor-general of Montana. Both of us being enthusiastic explorers, it was with deep regret that I parted with him to descend the Columbia, hoping we would unite in an expedition to the Park the next year. But perverse fate otherwise ordered; a small party was suddenly organized, with him as leader, when he as usual acquitted himself to the satisfaction of all, who by unanimous vote gave his name to the highest peak within the Park.

The dangers and duties of a useful life, however, were rapidly closing. Exposure in the gases and storms of the Park, with efforts and anxiety for Everts in his thirty-seven days of peril, revived a lung disease contracted in the army.

But no loving wife or children greeted his return to Helena. Instead came tidings that after much of a summer spent in trying to reach him *via* Missouri River and Fort Benton, low water and hostile Indians compelled their return to Indiana. There, broken in health and spirit, utterly worn out by disease and exposure, he reached them during the winter, only to die in the arms of those he so tenderly loved.

Not the ties of kindred, but of principles, united him with the noble Washburn family of New England; and though heroic in life and noble in death, the fathomless cañon at the base, the brilliant snowy sides and rocky summit of Mount Washburn may perchance guide the tourist in the Wonder-Land long after all else of him shall be forgotten.

THE DYING MANDANS.

⁴⁷ "Oh, ghastly scene of horror!
 Oh, ghastly town of doom!
 No hope in dawn of morrow,
 No halo 'mid the gloom."

History is silent, tradition meagre and conflicting, as to the origin or early history of the Mandans; but the circular ruins of their earth-lodges in numerous deserted villages are proof positive of their former numbers and successive removals hundreds of miles up the Missouri River, constantly dwindling before their more savage and warlike neighbors to the mouth of the Big Knife River.

There Lewis and Clarke found a remnant of about two thousand of them in 1804, and subsequently Catlin, Irving, and others, who had enjoyed their hospitality, with pen or pencil heralded their fame; and there, while hemmed in their villages by the ever ferocious Sioux, they, together with other confederate villagers, were nearly exterminated in 1838 by the ravages of the smallpox, or by bathing, Indian-like, in the chilling waters of the Missouri, in the hope of checking the disease.

This is not the place to theorize, as others have done, of the origin; these stanzas faintly portray the fate of the most civilized of all the Northwestern Indian nations.

But, as being a subject of general and permanent interest, I, from personal knowledge, endeavor to describe the famous conical earth-lodge, which is conceded to have been the invention of this people.

First, a dry, commanding position is chosen, usually in the bend of a river, for both water and defence, and a strong stockade of log-pickets constructed across the neck. Then each group of kindred or friends excavate a ditch around a somewhat oblong circle, from forty to sixty feet in diameter, some two feet deep, and wide enough for material to make the floor to the circle or lodge perfectly level, which is beaten down very hard and smooth. Next, saving a space thereon four feet wide for a door-way, a compact row of posts is set in the ditch outside of, and leaning at an angle of ten to twenty degrees against, the bank of earth, rising about six feet above it, and a rough plate placed upon the top entirely around the circle. Then near the centre, four tall, strong crotches or posts with notches in the top are set, with timbers upon them, so as to leave a space four or five feet square for smoke-hole and window. Next, a compact layer of rafter-timbers, with the larger ends on the outside, and smaller ends on the centre plates, and middle supported and somewhat elevated by another row of posts and supporting timbers, having their cracks and crevices carefully calked with coarse grass and daubed with tough mud. Then against the outside posts a heavy bank of earth is thrown, and over the entire roof a foot or so of the alkali earth of the plains. This, with its natural tendency to pack, and being constantly occupied as a lookout-, romping-, and lounging-ground for Indians and dogs of all ages and sexes, soon becomes perfectly smooth, wind-, water-, fire-, and bullet-proof. In the centre is a depression for the fire, and around against the walls the family rooms, often tastefully partitioned by skins and blankets, and on the posts gaudy shields and other war weapons and ornaments. In these the rude bedsteads are formed by low crotches and cross-poles, each covered by a green buffalo-skin, hair up, which in drying stretches very smoothly, and with abundance of robes and blankets forms a welcome bed, never forgotten by a weary or wounded trapper in a hospitable Mandan lodge as of old. Villages thus built around a central court for gossip, dance, and council are worthy of a patent, and any civilized land would have long since been plastered with them; and though the invention of a rude people in a prehistoric age, so nicely do they meet their requirements of climate, surroundings, and safety, that a rude chimney and an occasional small window, when near the whites, are all the improvements attempted since I have known them; and, in fact, the earth-roof is now in nearly universal use by the whites throughout all those arid regions.

THE DYING TRAPPER.

⁴⁸ "Hard by those spouting fountains,
　　Far, oh, far away!
　Done with his frays and scoutings,
　　A dying trapper lay."

These stanzas are a heartfelt tribute to the memory of a trapper comrade, who fell and died beside me, as therein portrayed, near a spouting fountain in a lonely glen of the, as then called, "Big-horn Mountains," east of the Yellowstone Lake, in the days long agone; and the words of the second line of each verse are, so far as I am aware, the only ones in the English language which rhyme with the Ab-sa-ra-ka Burial Refrain.

BOZEMAN BOLD.

⁴⁹ "Bull-boat and raft, mustang and mule."

Bull-boat is an Indian craft peculiar to the turbid sandbar rivers of the treeless plains, where swarming with buffalo, and are thus constructed:

The hair and flesh are removed from a green buffalo-hide which has not been severed, or has been reattached between the upper portion of the hind legs. This is then stretched very tightly over circular hoops and connecting ribs of willow or other light brush or small poles, and, being thus allowed to dry, forms a circular boat from four to six feet in diameter and nearly two feet deep, or in a form not unlike a huge flaring-topped cheese-box or a monster, very flat-bottomed, potash-kettle.

They are sometimes made of two hides, well attached with elk, beaver, or buffalo sinews, and are then relatively larger. They have little steerage, but, in border jargon, "heaps, heaps of float," and are so tough that they are seldom stove on rocks or snags, and so buoyant as to whirl around or glide over snags, sand-bars, or obstacles liable to wreck nearly any other known craft, as I well know from personal experience, having at various times in them descended nearly all of the mighty rivers of the great plains.

With all these advantages they are so light that, after a brief drying in the sun and wind, the lusty pack-horse squaw of a lazy village Indian brave will dexterously toss one of these boats inverted over her head, and with it speedily regain upon the banks the distance lost in the oblique descent of crossing the wide and foaming Missouri or the Yellowstone.

This is but one of the many inventions of man for utilizing the provisions of nature in surmounting peculiarities of these regions seemingly unsurmountable.

50 "War-path ford of Crow and Brule."

An ancient ford of the Yellowstone near the confluence of the Shields River, below the gate of the mountains, famous in all legends of Indian and border warfare.

51 "Sure, phantom-warriors caused the doom."

There is no question as to the date or the place of Bozeman's death, which was in 1868, upon the south bank of the Yellowstone River, a few miles below its gate of the mountains. But the versions regarding the premonitions and reputed vision of his family, and the warning of his death, which are said to have caused the stoic indifference with which so famous a scout and fearless Indian-fighter met his fate, are singularly conflicting.

The version which, in the light of subsequent events and reputed dying confessions of some of the participants, differs somewhat from that current when I was there soon after his death, and which was literally followed in penning this poetical tribute to his deeds and death.

THE CLOUD-CIRCLED MOUNTAINS.

52 "My heart's in the mountains," etc.

These stanzas were originally published as the close of an address to the patrons of the "Norris Suburban," upon my leaving for the Wonder-Land in 1877.

WHERE ELSE ON EARTH?

⁵³ "Where else on earth does water furnish
Rocky evidence so strong
Of its power to build and burnish,
As this terrace, high and long?"

The Terrace Mountain in the National Park, which is two miles in length, nearly one thousand feet high from the valley of the west fork of the Gardiner River above, and more than two thousand feet from the cañon of the main Gardiner below it, all of which has apparently been formed by the terrace-building springs, of which the famous Mammoth Hot Springs, whence we supply our table, bath-houses, and irrigate our garden at the headquarters of the Park, is only the dwindling remnant.

⁵⁴ "Long its waves, by tempest driven,
Fiercely lashed its seething shore."

Doubtless true, as the shore-line terraces of the ancient lake are still plainly traceable upon the sides of the Terrace Mountain and of Bunsen's Peak.

⁵⁵ "Then the ever-lashing billows
Rent a gap in mountain-side."

This monster erosion in the side of Bunsen's Peak, and the yawning impassable cañon of the west fork of the Gardiner, between it and the Terrace Mountain, are in plain view from the balcony of our headquarters at the Mammoth Hot Springs, three miles distant.

⁵⁶ "Hence these ruins weird and fearful,
And the cliffs so white and grand."

With a clear-cut outline against the sky, the vertical snowy-white walls of the calcareous marbleized ancient Hot Spring deposits rise many hundreds of feet above the successive miles of the angular débris along the Gardiner below, of the cause or magnitude of which the casual observer will form no adequate conception.

Only by days of rugged dangerous cliff-climbing upon and beneath the Terrace Mountain, near the Rustic Falls, and along the foot of the white cliffs, can a tourist obtain even a superficial knowledge of the gigantic scale upon which frost, fire, and flood have alternately built up, fractured, and eroded this region. Within a distance of four miles from our headquarters, and mainly within plain view thereof, are the summits of Bunsen's Peak, as well as of the Everts, Terrace, and Sepulchre Mountains, the yawning cañons of the Three Forks and main Gardiner Rivers, five cataracts, many interesting cascades and rapids, and the grandest evidences of both ancient and modern terrace-building springs known to earth.

In addition to the descriptions of all the scientists who have visited the terrace-building springs, a brief review of my own observations and theory recording them may be found on pages 13-16 of my report of 1879.

BRADLEY THE BRAVE.

⁵⁷ "Last of a race of warriors who served their country well."

Lieutenant James Bradley was a young but daring Union scout in West Virginia during the three months' service of 1861, and subsequently served with distinction under his father, Colonel E. D. Bradley, of the Sixty-Eighth Ohio Volunteer Infantry, until the close of the Rebellion.

He then entered the Seventh Regiment United States Infantry, and served with marked ability, courage, and success upon the border, until, in leading the charge of General Gibbon's Big-Hole fight with Chief Joseph, he was the first white man killed, and was buried amid the valley-willows of the field.

⁵⁸ "And green o'er thy grave twine the myrtle and laurel."

A heartfelt desire that his bones might thus rest beside his heroic kindred in the Christian land of his birth.

Alas! as shown in the stanzas called "The Warrior's Grave," which were subsequently written, these hopes are not to be realized, but, instead, the rank weeds and willows still droop over his vacant grave, and his bones, commingled with those of his foes, doubtless still bleach upon the slaughter-field of the far-distant mountain where he fell.

FROM BIG-HORN'S BLEAK MOUNTAINS.

⁵⁹ " From Big-horn's bleak mountains white glistening with snow,
The Big-horn's bright fountains through green meadows flow."

Romantically and enchantingly true of the, to me, personally well-known valley and its countless timber-fringed streams descending from the snowy bordering mountains, and meandering amid the long, rolling coteaus to their confluence with the river, and of that in the dim outline of the horizon with the mighty Yellowstone.

These lines were inspired by a distant field-glass view of this matchless landscape from a lofty peak of the Sierra-Shoshone range during the explorations of 1881.

⁶⁰ " Till Custer from Rosebud saw valley as sweet."

Or rather from the summit of the divide to the Big Rosebud River, as distinct from the Rosebud confluent of the Still-Water at the present Crow Indian Agency.

This is far west of the Big-horn River, while Custer descended a streamlet from the east to his last battle upon the eastern or Little Big-horn (now called Custer River) fork of the Big-horn River, twenty miles above their confluence, near which Fort Custer has since been constructed.

⁶¹ " And Farrer and comrades."

Colonel Farrer, now of Mount Clemens, Michigan, who led the remnant of the Big-horn expedition of 1870 safely, bringing in the famous Big-horn gun or mountain-howitzer to Bozeman late in that season.

THE GRANGER SONG.

⁶² " Oh, my rural friend and neighbor,
If inclined to roam."

These stanzas are the portion in rhyme of an address written by request for the Granger Clubs of Michigan, when many persons, to escape the hard times attending a period of financial depression, were rashly rushing from their peaceful homes in a wild crusade for gold amidst the hostile savages of the Black Hills and Big-horn Mountains in 1877.

BORDER BRAVE.

⁶³ "Not unavenged, for Looking-Glass."

This is the name of the famous Nez-Perce chief and favorite counsellor of Chief Joseph, who was killed in the decisive Woody Mountain fight.

THE TATTOOED ARTIST.

⁶⁴ "I sing of an artist, scribe, poet, and seer,
A lover of nature and scoffer at fear."

This poem has a substantial basis of fact, as may be attested by the hero, if living, as well as by many eye-witnesses of that enthusiastic but somewhat visionary pilgrim correspondent's sketching trip from a Missouri River steamer, long since the days of Catlin. Although the puncture, paint, and singing, as well as the nude gantlet running over cactus, cur, and breech-clout, are, with poetic license, somewhat exaggerated, still they were ample for our artist, and no further acquaintance desired with his Indian friends and their families at home. Indeed, sudden, radical, and lasting changes in the opinions of eastern tourists upon their forming the acquaintance of Mr. Lo and his family at home are neither rare nor strange, as there is much to be learned and regretted upon the rival sides of the Indian question, both of which, in these legends and notes, it has been my purpose to faithfully portray, rather than to conceal or misrepresent.

It will be observed that the Indian words used in this torture-chant are not wholly Da-ko-tian, but those of other tongues or jargons which seemed best calculated for the rapid reiteration peculiar to all Indian songs in their circling dances. The literal rendition of these songs in English is extremely difficult, if not impossible, because of the construction of their sentences, which read backwards, as the thirteenth line in the first Indian chant, "Wi-ta-wa-ta (ship) sa-pa (black) wan (one)," or "ship black one," is, in English, one, or "A black ship."

For the symphony of versification license is also taken in the accent of syllables, as Wa′kan, which is thus transferred from the second syllable to the first, as usually spoken by the white men.

THE MOSQUITO.

⁶⁵ " Like hornet hordes aroused to fury,
They greet us to their home."

Prominent in the journals of all explorers, travellers, and navigators since and including those of Lewis and Clarke are their execrations upon the mosquito tormentors of the Missouri and the lower Yellowstone.

To those pestiferous insects, by whom, despite a turf-smudge, thick gloves, mosquito-net, and head-gear, I was nearly devoured near Fort Buford while penning these lines, are they feelingly, if not affectionately, dedicated.

FRIGHTENED HANS.

⁶⁶ " The shining sands of coteaus reflecting heat like glass."

This, as is well known, is caused by the action of the constant and often high winds of those regions in carrying along all the finer and lighter portions of the soil, thus polishing like a mirror the upper surface of the pavement-like coating of those which remained.

"Mirage of gushing fountains dispel their frantic fears."

Few earthly views are as enchantingly beautiful or as fatally alluring as are the mirage-built phantom groves, lakes, and meandering streams to the thirsty, parched, and panting pilgrim upon the treeless prickly-pear plains or grease-wood, alkali deserts of the mighty West.

Nor are these phantoms, in accordance with popular belief, always seen inverted, but often in their natural position, and so lifelike and real that only the practised eye of the rover will perceive that even the lakes and streams are not depressed beneath, but slightly elevated above, the real horizon, hanging, as it were, in the air, with a thin, hazy outline of the earth's surface barely perceptible beneath them.

[67] "Fear of scalding led to roasting on the fated Yellowstone."

The narrative of the wanderings of Hans and family, his scalding, fright, and Teutonic ejaculations at the hot spring in the Gallatin Valley, as well as their wild stampede and speedy massacre by the Indians upon the Yellowstone, are all substantially true, thus only leaving their death by the ancient Indian mode of roasting not well attested, and hence inferentially chargeable to poetical license by the author.

AFAR FROM THE CITIES AND HAMLETS OF MEN.

[68] "Afar from the cities and hamlets of men,
I follow the streamlet through forest and glen ;
The elk with proud antlers enlivens the bowers,
And brilliant and fragrant the meadows with flowers."

It is believed that the accuracy of this description of the broad, grove-dotted valley of Cascade Creek above its last cañon and falls will ever be conceded by any candid observer.

Equally true was the presence of the then docile elk and deer in fabulous numbers when my old comrade, Frederick Bottler, there, with seven rapid discharges of his unerring rifle, killed five huge antlered elk, as, under the title of "The Successful Hunter," is immortalized in one of the artist Jackson's photographic views of the Hayden Geological Exploration of 1872.

[69] "As thunders from heavens unclouded I hear."

A feeling of awe (perhaps partially superstitious) difficult to escape, explain, or even describe, is felt, when reaching the dark pine-fringed summits of the divide upon the trail from the open meadows of the cascade, upon a bright, cloudless summer's day one emerges at once into full view of the halo-fringed clouds of mist, and into hearing of the heavy booms of the cañon-hidden triple falls and roaring rapids of the Mystic River, the latter ever varying in volume and cadence, and the former in their form and brilliancy of coloring with the direction or velocity of the balmy mountain breeze.

> [70] " Adown to the lichens, mist-nourished and green,
> Where the floods as a deluge from heaven are seen."

As at other great cascades or cataracts, the showers of spray at the Great Falls of the Yellowstone nourish a carpet of moss and lichens of various forms and brilliant shades of yellow and green coloring, which form a dense but slightly adherent, and to the footsteps treacherous covering to the dripping rocks around them.

This I found dangerously evident upon the lower portion and nearly vertical and crumbling brilliantly red- and yellow-tinted walls of the Grand Cañon of the Yellowstone, upon my descent thereof alone in 1875.

This was from where our rustic bridge now spans Spring Creek, adown or near its jagged waterway to the river, a portion of which, by the subsequent dislodgment of a huge mass of the wall-rock at the Red Pinnacles, is now impassable.

The present route is along a rude pathway which I recently made from just above these pinnacles, directly across the face of the sliding shales, to a jutting point of crumbling rocks about five hundred feet directly below our now pole-railed Point Lookout, and thence by a rough, very steep, but direct descent of five hundred feet to the foaming river.

In small parties only should persons attempt this descent, as to the usual danger of a misstep and headlong descent to horrid death is the still greater one from dislodged masses or fragments of the crumbling wall-rock, which in velocity nearly and in danger fully equal projectiles from a park of artillery. This is now the nearest point of descent or of approach to the foot of the Great Falls upon the northwest side; but by rafting, or, in very low water, fording the river something less than a mile above the Upper Falls, or at them if the projected bridge be constructed, tourists will be able to reach the grove-capped cliff overlooking the Great Falls. Thence, by proper effort and care from crumbling rocks and slippery lichens, persons may safely descend to the river and as near to the foot of the Great Falls as the matchless rebound of the sheet of water from its nearly four hundred feet of vertical descent will allow, and where it is believed the poet's description of lichens, mist-clouds, and halos, as well as of "the floods as a deluge from heaven," will be verified and appreciated.

71 " Henceforth be my music the cataract's roar."

At the risk of seeming egotism, I would briefly note that these words differ more in form than in sentiment from those to be found in my printed "Journals of Rambles in the Far West" at the time of my first visit to these falls.

Nor have my subsequent encampments in the Glen of the Cascade, while making the bridge and other improvements above the Grotto Pool and Crystal and other falls, or at my other secluded haunts amid their commingled spray and thunders during Indian raids, lessened but rather increased my attachment for this rainbow-spanned refuge from the gilded haunts of fashion and pleasure, and the crafty wiles of the politician, the speculator, or the money-lender, in these days when proffered friendship is too oft a lure, and real friendship a cherished vision of the past,—in these enlightened but degenerate days, when far too often robbery and betrayal of public trusts are viewed and punished in inverse ratio to the magnitude of the crime and the numbers and position of the shares of the spoils, and man is prized less for his birthright as such, or for his principles and practices of true manhood, than for the wealth or the influence which by any means, ever so reprehensible, he may have acquired.

Hence my changeless attachment to these unpolluted scenes of the grandest handiwork of nature's God as a refuge alike in life, and in death a tomb, earnestly trusting that if in this wild region it be mine to fall, my final resting-place may be beneath the moaning pines and balsams of my chosen camping-grove whenever able to cross the river to reach it upon the southern cliffs, amid the spray, overlooking the Great Falls, that my unfettered spirit in its earthly visitations may be greeted by the scenes and sounds so appreciated and enjoyed while tenanting its transient refuge of clay.

OH, IS THERE IN THIS WORLD SO DREAR?

⁷² "In crumbling home of friends afar."

The ruins of the famous Baronet cabin, upon the high, huge granite boulder-strewn basaltic point above the confluence of the two forks of the Yellowstone River.

It occupied the site of one previously burned by the Indians, which (aside from the loop-hole, earth-roofed block-house of unknown builders, the ruins of which are referred to on page 7 of my official report of 1878) was the first residence known to have ever been constructed by white men within the subsequently dedicated Yellowstone National Park, and at few places, other than the regular battle-fields in all these regions, has there occurred more varied or thrilling scenes than within or around it.

⁷³ " Above the ceaseless dash and roar,
Where mountain torrents greet."

The forks of the Yellowstone River, forty miles below the lake and twenty below the Great Falls, upon its main fork, and where, only from these falls to the confluence of the Gârdiner River, a distance of fifty miles in the Grand Cañon of the Yellowstone, is there a wagon-route of approach to the stream.

Neither of these dashing mountain torrents are there ever frozen over; safely fordable, or even approachable, where the first, and for ten years the only, bridge ever crossed any portion of the mighty Yellowstone River, was built over the main fork, just above their confluence, by Jack Baronet and other Clarke's Fork miners in 1871.

This poem was inspired and partly written by the camp-fires when I was alone at this cabin in August, 1877.

I then found it only a haunt of howling beasts and screaming birds of prey, gathered upon the decaying bones and decomposing fragments of the flesh and hides of game left by Charley Reynolds and other friends, whose companionship I had there enjoyed in 1875, and from a soul-harrowing view of whose bleaching bones upon the Custer slaughter-field I had just returned.

Sad as were my feelings then, a forecast of the events soon to follow could have only darkened the shade.

Within one week from that time I passed that bridge, clinging to my horse, faint from the loss of blood from an accidental wound received at Tower Falls, and within one month thereafter the trail which I then followed to the falls of the Gardiner was dusty with the tramp of a portion of Chief Joseph's hostile Nez-Perces and their captured horses, and encrimsoned with the gore of their slaughtered owners; the bridge was partly burned by them in their matchless retreat, and the cabin was dismantled for material for its repair by General Howard, in his long, patient, and then misunderstood and misrepresented pursuit.

TO THE TIE AT HOME.

"Far away on the cliffs of this wild roaring river."

These stanzas, which doubtless evince more pathos than poetry, may be less esteemed by the public than the poet, from the circumstances under which they were written.

As noted in my journal, and published in my report of 1877, by the sudden sundering of a stirrup-strap I was precipitated from a bucking horse over a ledge of rocks, so seriously injuring my neck and spine as to compel me to return to the head of the falls of the middle fork of the East Gardiner, where I fainted from the loss of blood and over-exertion.

After recovering sufficiently to crawl to the brink and swallow a cupful of the delicious water, by painful effort I was enabled to make a rude couch of my blanket and some balsam boughs beneath the trees at the eastern end of where the bridge now spans the quivering brink of the falls.

There, while by weakness and the music of the falling waters lulled into semi-unconsciousness, the prelude and much of the poem was pencilled in my memorandum-book, hopeful that if, as then seemed probable, I should there perish alone, my remains might perchance be found and these lines reach her for whom they were intended.

THE WARRIOR'S GRAVE.

⁷⁵ " A mould'ring plate and headboard."

This is all that was found upon Gibbons's and Chief Joseph's battle-field of the Big-Hole Pass, which I could so fully identify as pertaining to the fated " Bradley the Brave" as to feel justified in conveying to his mourning friends.

This visit was made through deep snows from the Bitter Root Valley, some months after the publication of my tribute to his memory, and, alas! the bones of that friend of other days and scenes had been dragged from their shallow resting-place amid the willows, near where he fell, by ravenous beasts who still haunted the field.

At the time of my visit they nightly retramped the snow, and, in search for food, overturned the remnants of garments, blankets, and horse-hides, and in hideous revels more fully commingled the bleaching bones of fallen friend and foe.

BLAZE BRIGHTLY, O CAMP-FIRE!

⁷⁶ " Earth's treasures all vanished, no heaven to gain."

The immediate incentive for penning these stanzas was the jocular remark of a comrade of its being fortunate for him that, when he had once, within the space of a few months, squandered a fortunate stake, or placer find, of seventy-five thousand dollars, that it was not a hundred thousand, or he could not have survived the attendant dissipation.

This, and similar admissions of other comrades beside our cedar-sheltered camp-fires during a terrific mountain snow-storm, recalled painfully recollections of the needless failure and hopeless fall of kind, and some of them morally-reared and well-educated comrades gone, still destitute of graves, or filling only dishonored ones, all along my checkered pathway of wandering upon the border.

Hence these lines of pensive, mournful reflection are published, hopeful that they may beneficially recall in the really noble heart of some rough-clad mountaineer the scenes of his innocent childhood and guileless youth, the instructions of the week-day and the lessons of the Sabbath-school, the tender admonitions and parting prayers of loving kindred now peacefully slumbering beneath the willows in the consecrated cemetery of some distant Christian land.

UNION OF THE VALLEYS.

77 "For the ever-fickle river veered away to meet its mate."

A proverbial characteristic of the Missouri River is the ceaseless shifting of its muddy channel, which, by occurring at the point of its confluence with the Yellowstone, effected the channel at the fur-traders' old Fort Union above it, thus contributing to its abandonment and the subsequent construction of Fort Buford below the confluence.

78 "And the fort, its cache and lodges, were abandoned to their fate."

The bank of the Missouri River above Fort Union being very dry and easily excavated, has been from time immemorial a favorite cacheing site; and having assisted in making several there and many elsewhere, I will briefly describe the operation. This originally French word cache (usually pronounced cash), or hiding-place, has long been the universal and appropriate name for a deposit of corn, furs, blankets, or in fact anything a party desires to bury safely for another occasion, usually for concealment, but sometimes only for safety from the animals and elements. In horizontal layers of soft sandstone, like that near Fort Union, a place is selected where there is a foot or so of loose sand-covering, which is removed, and a circular hole large enough to admit a man is after a foot or so gradually enlarged to the desired size, shaped when completed much like a very low broad earthen jug. When the floor and sides are covered with a layer of dry brush or bulrush mats, or both, it is filled with the utmost care, that it may not settle and betray the site. The top is then crammed with hides, the mouth well filled with the removed rocks, the sand replaced, and every vestige of goods, rocks, etc., carefully removed in sacks or skins, and thrown, often several miles away, into a stream or lake. When thus completed, a camp fire over or near the mouth, with the usual tramping of men and animals, and a few hours of sand-drifting, so fully obliterate all trace that actual knowledge or digging alone will disclose it. When the site is a pure sand-bank, the cache must widen less and be better supported and packed; and if in a grove, a dry bush or a cedar or other hardy shrub, not soon wilting or changing color, even if dying, is most carefully cut around and lifted, with all the earth possible attached, upon a skin or blanket, and, when completed, replaced; and so well is all concealed in these vast regions, that I have little doubt fewer caches are actually found and robbed than are lost by the sudden removal or death of the owners.

The ruins of old Fort Union are still plainly traceable between the present earth-lodge village of the mongrel Indians and the long line of mainly abandoned caches along the sandy bluffs above it.

[79] "Oh, for bard to chant their requiem! Oh, for storied pen to save."

This is the language of a heartfelt desire, which above all else has cheered my untutored pen in tracing as well as I am able a few of the countless well-known incidents and legends of the border, hopeful that the basis and language of fact may somewhat atone for the want of plot and finish found in the polished works of fiction.

OH, FOR BARD TO TRULY TREASURE.

[80] "Oh, for bard to truly treasure
Border scenes of days agone!"

To a person reared upon the border and familiar with the thrilling scenes and trying reverses of a life among the animals and aborigines of the plains, the deserts, and the mountains of what was then truly the pathless unknown West, the sincere but erroneous eastern sentimentalism regarding the Indian upon one hand, and the less humane but more practical opinions of the western pioneer upon the other, offer food for mature reflection, a broad field for the gleaning of facts, and ample scope for marshalling and recording them in authentic history by an abler pen than mine.

18*

But time is invaluable; the fiat of fate has gone forth that the onward march of the race of resistless destiny is to mould or annihilate all along its pathway; that the wild man and the wild beast shall alike become civilized or domesticated and useful in a practical age of progress if they will, and be exterminated if they will not.

Hence the constant evidence that the blood-curdling war-whoop, the defiant battle-rally, the rifle-ring, dying scream, and, alas! the sickening scalp-dance of to-day are replaced by the peaceful music of the woodsman's axe or the blacksmith's forge and factory whistle, the lowing of domestic flocks and herds, or the gleaner's carol around the peaceful homes and crowded school-rooms of to-morrow.

The spouting heart's-blood and festering flesh, alas! of fallen ones upon the gory fields of death of the season past fertilize the growing plant upon the harvest-fields of gladdening grain of that to come, for the use of a people who cease from their labors, and at the cheering peals of the Sabbath bell congregate in their steepled churches, to return thanks for the countless blessings of earth and the priceless promises of Heaven.

And hence, sternly but unregretfully, the polished ploughshare of human progress shall be driven rough-shod and relentless alike over the deserted village-sites and decaying bones of a race hesitating to enlist under its floating banner and keep step to its marching music.

The generation of the path-finding, death-daring planters of civilization and their paint- and plume-bedecked warrior opponents is rapidly gliding away; and if this duty of gathering and truthfully recording incidents of the border be neglected until the actors are fled, ere long they will be known only in the unreal sensation-tales of dime novels or yellow-covered literature, or else merged in the wild legends of mingled fact and fiction, of truth and romance, to swell the volumes of unreliable future history, which might have been authentic.

RUSTIC BRIDGE AND CRYSTAL FALLS.

<blockquote>
81 "Will these feet that trip so lightly
O'er this structure rude but strong."
</blockquote>

These stanzas were pencilled, read, and dedicated September 4, 1880, to the first party of tourists who crossed the then unfinished bridge over the Grotto Pool and Crystal Falls, a sketch of which may be found on page 21 of my report of 1881, and also with this poem.

Names of the persons comprising the party: Mrs. G. W. Monroe, Mrs. W. J. Beal, Miss Mamie Evans, Miss Mamie Langehorne, Miss Prudence Burchard, Miss Nettie Ray, Mr. Jack Baronet, Mr. George Miles, Mr. Walter Burleigh, Mr. David Roberts.

Of these persons Jack Baronet was the guide; George Miles, of Miles City, upon the Lower Yellowstone, is a nephew of the gallant fighting general N. D. Miles, and the others were residents of Bozeman, Montana Territory, or their friends.

HIGH TOWERS THE CRAGGY SUMMIT.

[82] "And beavers build their wiek-e-ups where warm the waters flow."

As may be found in the Glossary, wickeups is the Sho-shone Indian name for the conical hollow brush-heap often used by them for a summer dwelling, and by the pigmy Pi-utes and Digger Indians of the Humboldt and other greasewood alkali deserts at any season of the year where no cave in the rocks or lava-beds are convenient, and they are not too lazy or too busy in securing a food-supply of berries, crickets, and lizards to build one.

These are all of one story, while those of the beaver are of two, one of which is partially and the other wholly above water, and, saving the size, is in all respects the better and more permanent structure, and the occupants far more ingenious, industrious, and provident.

The favorite haunts of these animals are the tepid dam-obstructed outlets of many of the hot-spring basins, which are seldom frozen over so as to obstruct their use as canals for the floating of their supplies of willows or other wood, upon which or the bark of it they mainly subsist.

[83] " Gigantic wrecks of forests, all fossilized to stone."

In the face of the usually nearly vertical cliffs, more than two thousand feet high, fronting the Soda-Butte and the east fork of the Yellowstone River, near their confluence, may be seen as plainly as in bas-relief countless trunks of the primeval forest-trees, still erect as they grew, or prostrate as they were crushed, buried, and fossilized in the successive or alternating deposits of submergence and enormous overflow of oozy volcanic mud and slime. The long horizontal lines of demarcation between the various deposits are clear and distinct, and some of them so thin that the silisified trees (which were mainly diverse from those now growing in the Park, and in size fairly rivalling those of the Pacific coast) must have extended through and above them.

Startling as is this theory of the successive alternations of submergence, oozy overflow, forest growths vertically, the roots of one above or in place of the tops of that beneath it, and seemingly incredible the hypothesis, yet it devolves upon future geological research to disprove surface indications and establish a better one.

As many of these trunks, both erect and prostrate, are in sections containing caskets lined with beautiful amethyst and other crystals, the fossil-forests alone, of the countless marvels of the Wonder-Land, are to the scientist and the nation worth the cost of the dedication, protection, and opening routes of access to all of them.

[84] "All nature seems in contrast, in beauty, size, or awe,—
Creation, growth, and *ruin*, the universal law!"

Literally and proverbially true of nearly every portion, feature, and marvel of the people's Wonder-Land.

LONELY GLEN.

[85] "'Tis lion's scream resounding."

The midnight screams of a cougar, or mountain-lion, echoing from the cliffs to my lonely camp-fire in the glen just above the Great Falls of the Yellowstone, where one member of a party of tourists was killed, others wounded, and all of their animals and outfit captured by the hostile Nez-Perces in 1877.

REYNOLDS'S DIRGE.

⁸⁶ "My fagots were ruins of teepee, and tent,
  'Mid war-robes and blankets all gory and rent."

Literally true, at the camp-fire of myself and Baronet, upon the site of the hastily abandoned Indian village just below Reno's valley field.

From this, as referred to in the note to Gallant Charley Reynolds, we escaped in the twilight to a little grove of cottonwoods in a deep wash-out of the plains, five or six miles towards the Big-horn, and then cooked and ate a slight supper nearly under the trees then supporting the remains of several blanket-robed braves, who were doubtless killed or mortally wounded in the Custer or Reno fights.

Hence we proceeded cautiously some miles farther towards the Big-horn, and bivouacked until morning, meanwhile securing such sleep as we could obtain, each with a hand holding one end of the lariat of his grazing horse, with the stars for his canopy, blanket-covered cactus for his couch, and saddle for his pillow.

For a mountaineer I am not deemed superstitious; but from the proximity of the bones of my comrade Charley of a few months preceding, then attached to the cantle of my Spanish saddle, the fervid imagination of nerves overstrained amid the recent harrowing scenes, or merely the flickering phantoms of a poet's vision, the incidents of the dirge were conjured, and at the dawn the last verse was hastily written, the first being subsequently prefixed.

---

[87] IN CABIN, CAMP, OR COUNCIL.

The poem dedicated to General H. D. Washburn with the accompanying notes explains our nearly life-long acquaintance and friendship, and hence desire that my explorations in those regions should be commemorated by the second peak of Mount Washburn, rather than the first of the Gallatin range, which I explored in 1875.

During October, 1878, accompanied by the daring mountaineers Adam Miller and George Rowland, by dangerous cliff-climbing in the snow along the terribly-broken brink of the Grand Cañon, I turned the northernmost and far the worst spur of Mount Washburn, and camped in a clump of pines and balsams, upon one of the larger trees of which our record may still be found.

This is one-fourth of a mile easterly and several hundred feet below where our Grand Cañon trail now crosses the spur in Rowland's Pass, which alone I discovered, explored, and named the same evening, while Miller shot an elk and Rowland used a portion of the flesh in the preparation of our welcome evening's repast.

Beside this camp-fire amid the snow, exhilarated by the first successful effort of scaling this spur of Mount Washburn by white men of which I have any knowledge, and justly confident that we had found a new and valuable route between the snowy mountain-crest and the yawning cañon-brink, these few lines of, as I then believed, correct dedication of these towering peaks were written.

The subsequent discovery that Prof. F. V. Hayden had meanwhile very properly commemorated the visit, in 1874, of the famous Scottish traveller and writer, the Earl Dun-Raven, and transferred my name from that now called Bell's Peak, of the Gallatin range, to the one which still retains it towards the Goblin-Land, I cheerfully acquiesced; but the pith of the poem vanished, and is published only in connection with historical facts deemed more valuable.

THE ARTIST STANLEY.

[88] "But 'Uncas' and 'War-path' and 'Signal' shall stay."

These are the names of some of the few paintings, now chromos, which were saved from the general destruction of the artist Stanley's famous gallery of Indian paintings by an accidental conflagration in a room of the Smithsonian Institution in Washington, where they had been placed for safety, exhibition, and sale during the war of the Rebellion.

BURIAL TEEPEE.

⁸⁹ "The Ab-sa-ra-ka chieftain most bravely fighting fell."

The famous Long-Horse, chief of the Absaraka, or Crow, nation of Indians, who fell and was entombed in a magnificent war-teepee, as portrayed in the poem, which was written upon my visit to his burial teepee and of the place of conflict soon after his death in 1875.

BOLD TRAPPER OF THE CAMP-FIRE.

⁹⁰ "Bold trapper of the camp-fire."

Jones Whitney, a youthful trapper comrade along the great lakes and in the wilds of Northwestern Ohio.

He there married, and soon after removed with his family to the Walla-Walla Valley in Oregon. There, by the assistance of a faithful Indian friend, he escaped one of the border massacres, and in a long and perilous journey, with the snowy crest of Mount Hood as a guide by day, and the stars by night, ultimately reached the Dalles of the Columbia in safety, where he settled, prospered, and, after repaying in the East my visit of 1870, died, a wealthy and esteemed Christian citizen.

The ties of early association in jointly sharing the perils of border-life by day and the weary watch by night are dearer and as enduring as those blood akin; nor will any of the bent, bald, or grizzled remnant of the early path-finders fail to understand, and perchance appreciate, this border mode of expressing regret for comrades gone, or the blending of trails and camp-fires in some mountain glen or sheltered park of that hoped-for better land.

THE WARRIOR'S DIRGE.

⁹¹ "Gone, brave brother, gone from the suffering and strife."

Brevet Colonel Thomas B. Weir, captain of the Seventh Regiment of United States Cavalry, died suddenly of congestion of the brain at his recruiting station in New York City soon after his return from the disastrous campaign of the Little Big-horn in 1876.

CYPRESS SHADOWS.

⁹² " Where the long reeds quiver, where the pines make moan."

This fitting requiem beneath the plaintive moan of the waving pine-tops at the silent burial, without religious ceremony, or a burial-casket of an emigrant's child beside a malarial bayou in the sterile pine-knobs of Northeastern Minnesota, came like electric flash along nearly forty years of fading reminiscences of kindred scenes in the Calumet Desert at the head of Lake Michigan. Such scenes are, alas! ever too frequent among the poor but worthy pioneers of civilization, who brave the diseases and the dangers of the border hopeful of a quiet home in their old age and of benefiting the children.

I'VE TRAILED THE PROUD COLUMBIA.

⁹³ " And here I pause and ponder at trace of friend of old."

William Turnage, in all those regions only known by his sobriquet, "Shirt-collar Bill," the famous scout, guide, and packer, with whom I visited the Steptoe and other battle-fields of the great Oregon Indian war of 1856; and we by ourselves encamped a night beneath the basaltic walls of the deeply-eroded cañon of the Peluse, between its mouth at Snake River and its sacred falls, seven miles above, in 1870. We slept in our blankets only, among the bleaching bones of the numerous pinto and coyuse horses, which died of their wounds, of starvation, or were slain for food by the remnant of the whites, while here for many weeks hemmed in by the victorious Indians after the Steptoe defeat, and where, in the days of close fighting with knife, hatchet, and bows and arrows, or at best mainly with short-range, muzzle-loading, flint-lock guns, which, from the liability of the powder to flash in the pan, were never a reliable gun at vertical firing, the incidents are said to have occurred substantially as related in the poem.

HO, WAKEN!

⁹⁴ "Ho, waken, you dwellers in chambers of clay,
  Arise from your slumbers and welcome the day!"

These lines are an imaginary address to a group of skeletons which I found in a walled-up timber- and cement-covered vault in the base of a great earth-mound on the commanding bluff above East Dubuque, Illinois, during my past season's ethnological researches in the Mississippi Valley. The oak-timber ceiling was so decayed as to have fallen in, but the cement or dried-mortar roof was still intact, and the skeletons of six adult persons, four children, and one infant, the latter in its mother's fleshless arms, were mouldering from a sitting posture in a circle around sea-shell dishes, weapons, and utensils of stone, fragments of pottery, and rude shell-ornaments.

⁹⁶ "And whose is this dust in these chambers beside?"

Each end of the vault was partially walled off, and contained several bushels of very fine cremated human dust, brought and thus carefully garnered from some unknown and perhaps distant locality; although several of this group of mounds which I opened in 1857, and others near Prairie du Chien, Wisconsin, during the past season, were unmistakably cremation-mounds above the skeletons of persons carefully buried in the earth beneath them.

⁹⁶ "And why are these ramparts so lofty and long
  Widespread o'er the plains where the antelope throng?"

This group of mounds is near the southern border of the famous Effigy mounds of Wisconsin, the beasts, birds, and reptiles of which, including the so-called Elephant Mound, one hundred and forty-six feet in length, are along the Mississippi uniformly headed southward.

NORTHERN CLIME.

⁹⁷ " Faint I recall, through mists of time."

This poem is intended less as the description of any one trip to the pathless Northwest than of the usual incidents attending all of them, as well as the tragic fate of the participants, not one of whom that ascended the Saskatchewan, so far as I am aware, is now living. In fact, the sole survivor of those early trapper and trader friends, even those who did not cross the British line with the Hudson Bay traders, is the energetic, ever-temperate, moral, honorable, and now esteemed and honored ex-State-senator D. W. H. Howard, now of Wauseon, Fulton County, Ohio, to whom none of the too often just denunciations of the border trader in any sense apply.

DE SOTO.

⁹⁸ " Damp was the day and dreary, the night was dark and cold;
Worn were my limbs and weary, my refuge hovel old."

The incidents in these lines truthfully-portrayed in connection with the production of this historical poem were thus preceded and followed. Of my ethnological work during the past season were researches of the famous flat-topped mounds, earthwork enclosures, and unique pottery-filled cemeteries of a supposed prehistoric people along the Southern bayous, lakes, and rivers. Commingled with these, from the foot-hills of the Ozark Mountains in Missouri and Arkansas, at various places along the Black, White, and notably the St. Francis Rivers below the "sunk lands" of the great earthquake of 1811 and '12, as well as from Memphis to Napoleon along the Mississippi, and much of the country visited beyond it, are detached earthworks, popularly believed to be the work of De Soto and his followers during their years of wanderings in these regions nearly three centuries and a half ago. One of these is near Helena, another where it is claimed their brigantines were built, at Old Town, thirty-five miles (by the river) below in Arkansas, and another in Mississippi, nearly opposite the latter, but somewhat back from the river, near the fine residence and hospitable home of the brothers J. and J. G. Carson, which they have constructed upon the circular acre of flat summit to an ancient mound fully twenty feet high. While engaged in researches of this and similar mounds adjacent, I spent the day and night preceding, and the forenoon of Christmas, 1882, there finding and partially perusing a brief narrative of De Soto's wanderings and death, being the first connected record of them which I had ever seen. Christmas afternoon I rode six miles to Frier's Point, crossed the skiff-ferry to Westover, and finding no better mode that night, in a rude dug-out mule-trough as a canoe, aided by a colored man, and my spade as a paddle, descended the Mississippi ten miles, and obtained such board and lodging as I could at Old Town, now reduced to a residence and a rum-hole, such as they are.

Although there are some fine ranches along the shores of Long and Old Town Lakes, which naturally outlet here, I was unable during the holidays to obtain help in the severe but successful labor of opening ancient mounds and earthworks, and securing human skeletons, unique pottery, and other interesting relics. With health seriously impaired by a direct transfer from years of duty in the cool, bracing Northern air at the fountain-heads of this mighty river to the malarious fogs of the Southern cypress-swamps and bayous fully four thousand miles adown it, and unable to obtain a guide or horse, I returned from an arduous day's effort in measuring and sketching some large and interesting ruins in the cane-brakes six miles towards Modock, wet, weary, and seriously ill. There, in my rude depository of relics, without fire, light, or window, with strangely blended thoughts of my cheerful distant home, of the ancient occupants of the place, the embarkation of Moscoso's remnant of De Soto's band, and the fate of both, I sought unrefreshing slumbers, from which I was startled by the brief tumult of a descending steamer and the howling of a transient winter's storm. Shivering in the dreary dawn, this record of my night's vision was commenced, continued at intervals in the measurements of the works attributed to Moscoso during that day, and concluded upon that following, while in an old abandoned cabin upon the opposite side of the river awaiting a steamer, and slightly reviewed in the pleasant cabin of the "Golden Crown" Ohio boat while ascending to Helena. It was then laid aside during my subsequent researches along the Yazoo and Sunflower Rivers, and now revised, and, together with this note of explanation, added to my volume of Legends now in press, as the sole contribution from a region pre-eminent in those which are thrilling, hopeful the poem is not too deeply tinted by the sombre shadows surrounding its couch of birth.

It is also earnestly hoped that no language of this poem will be thought to wantonly assail any nationality or religion. Surely the in part lineal descendant of the in many respects justly lauded " Pilgrims of Plymouth Rock," who frankly condemns their witch-burning, Quaker-expelling, and kindred acts of bigotry, intolerance, and persecution towards those of their own race in the very refuge to which they fled to escape it themselves, may be pardoned for recalling historical facts and wholesale pillage or slaughter of alien pagans in distant lands,—acts which were approved, lauded, and rewarded by prince and pontiff in the age of the actors, when professed religion was, alas! too often propagated alike beneath the Crescent and the Cross, with the Bible for a shield to the breast of one party, and potent arguments from the battle-axe, the scimiter, or the sabre to that of the other.

       99 " Amid the holly shadows, upon the gory plain,
          Uncoffined sleep and moulder two hundred sons of Spain." .

As the charming impression derived from a view of the deep-green foliage of a grove of moaning pines, adown a mountain slope, along a meandering stream, or upon a landscape of wintry snow, even so is the thrilling effect of a view of the glistening green leaves and brilliant red clusters of the low-branching holly, fringing the sluggish bayous, bordering the sombre-hued, moss-draped gigantic forests or the boundless savannas of the sunny South, while these evergreens are there as beautiful and as prized in the towns of the living or the cemeteries of the dead as are the matchless green and outline of the fragrant balsam in those of the frozen North. Hence the appropriateness of the holly-grove upon the slaughter-field of Mau-il-la, which was alike one of the most wanton and merciless slaughters of the innocent natives, and also terrible and far-reaching retributions upon the white invaders, of the long catalogue of the Indian battles of our country. The narrative shows that De Soto entered a thriving fortified town, with the chieftain a captive, and a long retinue of slaves loaded with nearly all of their ammunition, spare arms, camp equipage, and countless valuable pearls and other ornaments taken from the living or plundered from the graves of the dead, and that they left it a smouldering funeral pyre, alike of the two thousand five hundred defenders, and nearly all of their slaves, ammunition, camp outfit, and plunder, more than one-third of their number dead, and the most of the remainder wounded around it. So galling were his losses that De Soto, rather than continue his march one hundred miles to where he knew there were vessels and supplies awaiting him at (probably) Mobile, but where his reverses in fortune would also become known to the world, chose to conceal this knowledge from his followers; and turning his back upon all succor, without ammunition or supplies, followed a wandering life of rapine to a remorseful death and uncoffined grave at a now unknown locality beneath the turbid waters of the mighty river which he discovered. After nearly a year of wandering through Arkansas and adjacent regions, months of brigantine-building and terrible fighting and suffering, a remnant of the band under Moscoso reached a Spanish colony in Mexico, nearly five years after their landing in Florida, which was May 30, 1539.

Although many statements in the narrative of these wanderers seem too thrilling to be true, yet in my researches of ancient remains in those regions I found much to sustain and little to disprove their accounts, that without regard to who constructed the flat-topped mounds, the natives of De Soto's time certainly occupied them in the midst of hamlets of plaster-walled and thatch-roofed residences, protected by strong palisades and surrounded by extensive cornfields and gardens; and no statements of the poem are unsustained by the narrative of the first white explorers of any portion of the mighty Mississippi Valley.

GLOSSARY.*

DEFINITION OF INDIAN WORDS AND PROVINCIALISMS USED BY THE AUTHOR IN THE PRECEDING VOLUME OF LEGENDS.

A.

Ab'sa-ra'ka (Dakota).—Crow Indians. (See *Crow*.)
A-gim' (O-jib-wa).—Snow-shoe.
An-i-me'ki (O-jib-wa).—Thunder.
A-ras'trea (Chilian).—A rude mill propelled by mule- or water-power, for grinding gold with boulders.
A-rick'a-ree' (Pani). A tribe of Indians found along the Missouri River. The name is frequently abbreviated to Rick-a-ree, and sometimes even Ree. (See those names.)
As-sin (Chippewa).—Stone.
A-was'sa-da'ki (Chippewa).—Far beyond the mountains.

B.

Bad-lands.—Elevated, terribly eroded, and broken, sterile alkali plains or terraces.
Ban-ach.—From the Indian name Ban-nack (Pa-nai-tse), a tribe of Indians who formerly frequented the Yellowstone National Park, from the west.

---

* This glossary is not published as a classical, but as a practical and necessary accompaniment of this work of tales and legends, so largely abounding in Indian or border words, names, and phrases, and is believed to be at least as full and accurate as any of the kind of which I have a knowledge, or as is essential for a proper understanding of the incidents related in the work.

Bed-rock.—A miner's phrase for the real facts of a case or foundation of anything, from the gold being usually found upon the bed-rock in placer-mining.

Big-Hole.—A very large, open, and elevated park or valley and pass in the very crest of the Rocky Mountains, which nearly encircle it, upon the head of the Big-Hole branch of the Jefferson Fork of the Missouri River, near the Deer-Lodge, in Montana.

Big-horn.—The name of the larger variety of the wild mountain-sheep. Thus called from the enormous symmetrical horns of the adult males. The Big-horn Mountains, as well as the river of that name, with its various Horn branches, derive their names from the immense number of these animals frequenting those regions.

Bi'son—The fleet and wary, dark, curly-haired buffalo of the mountain parks.

Black-Feet.—An Indian nation embracing the Black-Feet, Blood, and Pigan tribes; formerly the most powerful, ferocious, and dreaded nation infesting the head-waters of the Columbia, Missouri, and Yellowstone Rivers.

Bloody-Knife.—A famous Ree or a Sioux Mandan warrior and guide for the whites. He was killed with Charley Reynolds in Reno's valley fight upon the day of the Custer massacre.

Bozeman.—A noted guide and rival of Bridger's as a mountaineer, who was killed by the Indians upon the Yellowstone. (See note 51.)

Brid'ger, James.—The most famous guide of the mountains and great plains of the past generation, and from whom Bridger's Fort, Pass, Lake, and several streams derive their names.

Brule.—A powerful and ferocious tribe of the Sioux or Dakota nation, frequenting the Black Hills.

Buck'eye.—Originally the name of the American horse-chestnut variety of timber, from the abundance of which, in Ohio, it became the provincialism or sobriquet of the State and its inhabitants.

Buf'falo.—The gregarious shaggy bison of the great plains. For convenience in versification these names are used interchangeably in this work.

Bull-boat.—A circular, flat-bottomed boat used upon the sand-bar rivers of the treeless great plains, usually made of one, but sometimes of two, green buffalo-bull hides. (See note 49.)

Butte (Pigeon-French).—A conical hill-remnant of erosion upon the great plains and terraced bluffs of its rivers and foot-hills of the mountains. When capped by a horizontal layer of harder rock they are called table-buttes.

C.

Cache (cash, French).—Hiding-place,—*i.e.*, the peculiar excavations in dry bluffs for the goods, trinkets, powder, and furs of the old traders, and now a cant word for hiding anything. (See note 78.)

Cac'tus.—A variety of this well-known thorny plant, called the prickly-pear, is the pest of the plains, as a pilgrim in attempting to crawl for a shot at a buffalo or an antelope will soon learn and long remember.

Cal'u-met' (O-jib-way).—The sacred Indian pipe of peace. (See note 1.)

Cal'u-met' Quarry.—Sacred quarry, in Pipestone County, Minnesota, near the border of Dakota.

Cam'ass (Nootka) of the Chi-nook jargon, named La'ka-mas' for the edible-bulb-root of a plant growing in fertile meadows in the Columbia River regions, and hence the numerous camass-meadows and streams.

Ca-noe'.—Properly an O-jib-way Indian boat, made by hollowing out a log, or by covering a light frame-work of cedar with birch-bark, but now also applied to an imitation of the latter covered with oiled canvas.

Cañon (Spanish).—A deep, narrow, usually eroded, and often impassable mountain water-way.

Cay-ou'ta (ky-o'ta, Spanish).—Properly the small and sneaking but voracious prairie-wolf, but the name is frequently applied to any variety of this animal.

Chet-woot' (Chi-nook jargon).—Bear.

Chi-nook' (Chi-nook jargon).—A general name for the Nez-Perce, Flat'head, Wal'la-wal'la, U'ma-til'la, and other cluck and whistling Indians of the Columbia, as well as their peculiar jargon.

Chip'pe-way' (Indian tribe).—See *O-jib-wa.*

Copper race.—Red men, or the Indian aborigines of the most of North America.

Counts, a coo.—A provincialism for the French word coup, for a stroke, blow, or notch, and in border parlance literally signifies adding a coup or coo-notch upon his tally-stick or gun-barrel list of human scalps, each of which counts equally; for the spouting heart's-blood of an innocent maiden or helpless infant will christen as many warriors as that of the bravest chieftain. The number of those entitled to become warriors or add a coo therefor being from three to five of the first who touch the corpse, in addition to the one who secures the scalp, none of whom may perchance be the actual slayer.

Crow.—An Indian nation consisting of the mountain and river tribes, the crafty occupants of the Yellowstone and Big-horn regions. (See *Ab-sa-ra-ka.*)

D.

Da-ko'ta.—The Indian name for the Sioux confederation of tribes, the most numerous and powerful of all of our aboriginal nations. Their name in the sign-language is represented by drawing the right hand from left to right across the throat; literally, cut-throat. (See *Sioux.*)

Dal'les.—A peculiar waterfall, combining the direct leap of the cataract, the skipping of the sant, or leaping rapids, and notably a broken line of falls sideways, often fronting each other, caused by the dislodgment of basaltic columns or other jointed bed-rocks, as at the dalles of the Columbia River. The name is not found in dictionaries, and is of doubtful origin, perhaps from the word dally, or delay in sport, which is very expressive of their appearance.

Deer-bleat.—A Chippewa Indian wooden tube, with a copper or brass tongue, used for calling the doe to her fawn, by imitating its cries when hidden, at the period when its tracks leave no scent.

Dig'gers.—The most degraded aborigines of the Humboldt and other alkaline deserts; so called from their habits of digging for the roots of plants, as well as for snails and lizards, upon which, or crickets and grasshoppers, they mainly subsist.

Dog-soldier.—The adult Indian males who have not counted a "coup" at the scalp-dance to christen them as warriors.

Du-luth'.—A famous French missionary, one of the first to visit the great lakes and Upper Mississippi River regions.

E.

Earth-lodge.—The famous circular Mandan lodge or dwelling. (See note 47.)

F.

Flat-head.—A tribe of Chinook Indians of the Bitter-root, Jacho, and other valleys of the Upper Columbia River. The name is derived from the ancient (now abandoned) custom of pressing the heads of their infants from front to rear, in the clamp-like head-gear of their hanging cradles, and is expressed in the sign-language by patting the upper part of the forehead or even top of the head,—*i.e.*, Flat-head.

Fossil forests, or primeval forests fossilized; literally true. (See note 83.)

G.

Gey'ser (Icelandic, *geysa*, to boil).—Spouting or spurting hot springs of several varieties, all of which are found in surpassing numbers, size, and beauty in the Wonder-Land, or Yellowstone National Park.

Goat.—The white or long-haired, web-footed wild sheep of the snowy mountain regions of Idaho and Montana Territories, and adjacent portions of the British possessions. (See note 7.)

Goblin-Land.—See *Hoo-doo;* also note 27.

Griz'-zly.—With the possible exception of the white polar bear, the largest and most ferocious variety of the species. The name is from the color and texture of the outer coating of their hair.

H.

Ha'lo.—Properly, a circle round the sun or moon; but in this work, as upon the border, the name signifies the areola around the column of hot water from the spouting geyser, or the inimitably beautiful oscillating rainbows in the mist-cloud above them, or of cataracts.

He'-kha-ka' (Da-ko-ta).—The antlered or male elk.

Hoo'doo.—A mountain and region of rocky goblin-forms near the Wonder-Land. (See note 30.)

How'-how'.—Jargon; corruption of the salutation "How are you?"

I.

Il′la-hi′ (Chinook jargon).—Country (my).
I-san′ (E-sòn, Santee).—Knife.
I-san (*Tan′ka;* E-sòn, Ton′ka).—Big-Knives; Americans.
Isk′ko-te-wa′bo (Chippewa).—Whiskey.

K.

Ka′ (Chippewa or O-jib-wa).—No.
Ka′kaw (Chinook jargon).—Crow or raven.
Kam′ook (Chinook jargon).—Dog.
Ke′new (O-jib-wa).—War-Eagle.
Ki′ji (ke′je, O-jib-wa).—Perfect.
Ki′ji-Man-i′tou (ke-je-Man-e-tou).—Perfect spirit; good God.
Kin′-ne-ko-nick′.—A plant used as a substitute for tobacco.
Kitch-i-gam′i (O-jib-wa).—Great water; lake; Lake Superior.
Kitch′i-mo′ko-man′ (O-jib-wa).—Big-Knife; American.
Ko-kosh′ (O-jib-wa).—Swine or their flesh; pork.

L.

La′ka-mas′ (Chinook jargon).—See *Cam-ass.*
Lake Pep′in.—A broad, placid expansion of the Mississippi River in Southern Minnesota.
Lar′a-mie.—A fort upon the north fork of the Platte River, long a famous outfitting point for gold-seeking pilgrims. Also the name of a town, county, river, and a very extensive and beautiful but elevated park called Plains, in Wyoming Territory.
Leaping Rock.—A famous tottering vertical fragment of the wall-rock of the Calumet Cliffs.
Li′on.—The mountain-lion, so called. A very large and ferocious variety of the panther, similar to the Mexican cougar, whose midnight screams startle like the Indian war-whoop.
Little-horn.—Properly, a western branch of the Little Big-horn River, but formerly applied to the entire branch, now called Custer River, upon the coteau bluffs of which he met his fate.
Looking-Glass.—The ablest of the Nez-Perces chiefs, who aided Chief Joseph throughout his matchless retreat, and fell in the coula-trenches of his last battle at the Woody Mountain, near the British line.

Lo′lo-lo′ (lue′-la-loo, Chinook jargon).—Conqueror.

Long-Knife.—White man, so called by the Indians from the swords of the military officers.

Loping-steeds.—Pintos, bronchos, cay-ouse, and mustang, half or wholly wild horses of the West, the natural and habitual gait of nearly all of which is a lope, or long, swinging, graceful canter, seldom equalled by the larger but less sure-footed and hardy blooded horses of the East.

Lovely River.—The Yellowstone, between its lake and Great Falls; a peculiarly appropriate name.

M.

Maiden's Leap.—Rocky cliffs upon the eastern shore of Lake Pepin, famous in Indian legends. (See note 15.)

Mak-wa′ (Chippewa).—Bear.

Man-dan′.—A famous tribe of village Indians. (See note 47.)

Man′i-tou′.—Thus Anglicized from the O-jib-wa. Man-i-to, mystery, or mysterious spirit; God; and in these legends is by poetical license for symphony pronounced Man-ee′ta.

Man′o-nim′ (O-jib-wa or Chippewa).—Wild rice.

Mar-quette′.—An early daring but devout missionary and explorer, from whom several towns and streams of Michigan derive their names.

Min′ne-ha′ha.—Laughing-Water. Name of a lovely waterfall near St. Paul, and also of the heroine of Longfellow's "Hiawatha," as well as of the Maiden's Leap at Lake Pepin, in the legend of "The Calumet of the Coteau." (See note 15.)

Min′ne-ke′wa (Santee).—Water-god.

Min′ne-o′la.—Legendary lover of Minnehaha.

Min′ne-o′pa.—A famous legendary warrior of the Coteau Indians.

Min′ne-tan′ka.—Mighty river; the Mississippi. Also a lake in Minnesota.

Min′ne-wa-kan (water-god).—Sometimes applied to a steamboat.

Min′ne-wa′wa (Longfellow).—Pleasant sounds, as of the summer breeze and the leaves of the grove upon the parched plains.

Min′ni (Da-ko-ta).—Water.

Mo′ka-man′ (Chippewa).—Knife.

Mos′mos (Chinook jargon).—Buffalo.

Mount′ain-cat.—The lynx, or largest variety of the short-tailed wildcat, being nearly as large and more ferocious than the catamount or panther.

Mountain-Gate.—The last cañon upon the Missouri, Yellowstone, and other rivers, through which they emerge from the snowy mountains to the relatively open valleys or plains.

Mus'tang.—The small loping horse of Texas and the great plains, usually half and often fully wild.

Mys'tic Lake " of Wonder-Land," as distinct from a lovely mountain-lake near Bozeman, Montana.

Mys'tic River.—The Yellowstone, the most of which, as well as its lake, were long only vaguely known from legends of the Indians or tales of the roving trappers of those regions.

N.

Na'tion.—A primitive people, consisting of more than one tribe, often of several or many, usually, though not always, confederate.

Nez-Per'ce (French).—Pierced nose. A famous nation of Chinook Indians.

Ni-ba' (Chippewa).—Water.

O.

Ob-sid'e-an Cliffs.—Cliffs of natural glass fronting Beaver Lake in the Yellowstone National Park.

O-de-o'na (Chippewa).—Village.

Og'i-ma' (Chippewa).—Chief.

O-jib-wa.—A powerful tribe of Indians of the Upper Mississippi and Upper Lake regions. (See *Chippewa.*)

Os'a-ga' (Chippewa).—Sauk Indian.

Os-su-a-ry.—Deposit of human bones.

P.

Pale-face.—White man.

Pam'pas.—A poetical license in applying the name to the prairies of the North as well as South America.

Pap-poose' (O-jib-wa).—Indian child.

Park.—A relatively broad, elevated mountain-girt valley, one or more of which are found upon all the streams of the Rocky Mountain region.

GLOSSARY.

Pem'i-can.—Deer-, elk-, or buffalo-meat dried, pounded, and mixed with tallow, marrow, or bear's grease.

Pil'grims.—A provincialism or border name for inexperienced miners, and, in a broader sense, the travelling new-comers, especially miners, of a western region.

Pin'to (Spanish).—Spotted. The famous spotted loping war-horse of the Columbia River Indians.

Plains, Great.—The elevated, treeless regions between the Rocky Mountains and the prairies, from the latter of which they greatly differ, notably in their short tufts of buffalo and other native grasses, often commingled with the prickly-pear and the sage-brush.

Pros-pect'er.—A roving exploring miner.

Q.

Que'u-que'u (Chinook jargon).—Circle, circle.

R.

Ranch.—Border farm, usually very extensive, and mainly for pasturage.

Ree.—Indian tribe. (See *Rickaree*.)

Red-Cloud.—A famous Sioux chieftain from whom the war at the close of the Rebellion was called, as he was the acknowledged leader of the hostile Indians.

Red men.—North American Indians.

Rick'a-ree'.—Indian tribe. (See *Arickaree*.)

Rov'er.—Trappers, traders, prospectors, and other wanderers of the border.

S.

Sa'cred Quar'ry.—Calumet Quarry. (See note 1.)

Sals'se.—Mud geysers.

Sa'pa (Da-ko-ta).—Black.

Sas'ka-shawn'.—Anglicized name for the River of the Rapids in British America.

Scalp'-dance.—As the name signifies, a dance over the scalps of fallen foes.

Sha (Da-ko-ta).—Red.

Ska (Da-ko-ta).—White.

Sheep.—Wild sheep of two varieties. (See note 7.)

Sheep-Eat'ers.—The poor, timid, and originally harmless aborigines of the Wonder-Land, so called from their habit of obtaining their main supplies of food and clothing by the slaughter of these animals.
Shun'ka (Da-ko-ta).—Dog.
Shun'ka-wa'kan (San-tee).—Sacred dog; horse.
Shun'tan'ka (Da-ko-ta).—Big dog; horse.
Shun-tan-ka-ti-pi.—Horse-lodge; big-dog house; barn.
Shun-to-ke-cha.—The other dog; wolf.
Si'oux' (Se'ou', Da-ko-ta).—Nation of Indians. (See note 5.)
Si'wash (Chinook jargon).—Male Indian.
Skoo'kum (Chinook jargon).—Brave.
Sun'-dance.—The courage-testing dance and tortures of the male Indian at the age of puberty.

T.

Tan'ka (ton-ka, Da-ko-ta).—Large; great.
Tau-rine.—Chieftain; Sitting-Bull; an Un-ca-pap-pa Sioux chieftain, leader of the hostile savages at the Custer massacre.
Tee'pee.—From the Dakota ti-pi, or skin-lodge, as distinct from the Chippewa mat or the Mandan earth-lodge. It is the to-tem war-lodge of the Blackfeet Indians, but the name is often used interchangeably with other skin-lodges.
Ter'race.—Remnants of eruption or erosion, and often of both, rising in long, horizontal, stair-like lines from many of the mountain-lakes and rivers.
Til'la-cume' (Chinook jargon).—Enemies.
Ti'tons.—Tee'tons.
To'tem.—Symbolic Indian name.

U.

Ute.—An Indian nation of several southern tribes.

W.

Wa'h (O-jib-wa).—An exclamation much as "there," "so be it."
Wa-kan' (wa-kon', Dakota).—Mysterious one.
Wa-kan'da (Kick-a-poo).—Mysterious being; God.
Wa-kan'sich'cha.—Bad mysterious one; devil, or whiskey.

Wa-kan'tan'ka.—Great Wakan; great mysterious one; God Almighty.
Wam'pum.—Strings of shell-beads.
Wan (Dakota).—One, a or an.
Wa'pa-ha (Dakota).—A hat or cap.
War-bon'net.—The famous ceremonial head-dress and streaming pendant, ornamented with war-eagle quills.
War-dance.—A grand dance of Indian warriors in full paint and feathers at the ceremonial unearthing of the hatchet and hurling it at the totem of their foes, while preparing for an expedition against them.
War-Ea'gle.—So called from the parti-colored quill-feathers which are the favorite ornament of the war-bonnet and other head-gear of an Indian warrior; and even a lone quill erect in the scalp-lock is highly valued.
War-whoop.—The piercing scream of the Indian warriors in battle, which is often modified to a prolonged vibrating howl, echoing with awful intensity in the dark pine- and cedar-fringed gorges of the mountains, and once heard can never be forgotten.
Was'-sa-mo'win (Chippewa).—Lightning.
Wa-wa (Chinook jargon).—Call.
Woolly-sheep.—The white wild sheep or goat of the Rocky Mountains.
Won-der-Land.—The Yellowstone National Park.
Wi-chen-yan-na (Dakota).—Girl.
Wick'e-up' (Sho-shone).—Brush-house. (See note 82.)
Win'-i-ban (O-jib-wa).—Gone.
Wi'ta-wa'ta (Da-ko-ta).—Ship or boat.
Wiz'ard (jargon).—An Indian medicine-man, sorcerer, or magician.

Y.

Yanc'tona or *Yanc'to-a.*—Northern tribe of the Sioux nation of Indians.

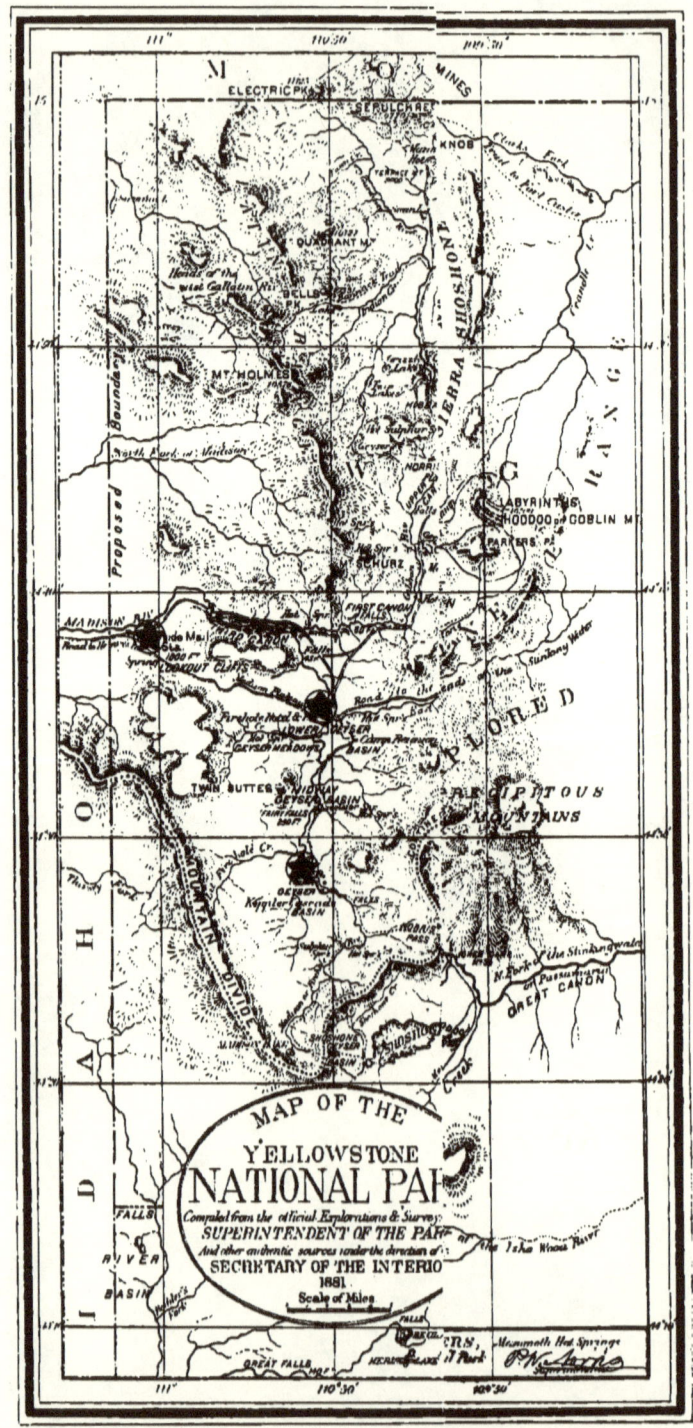

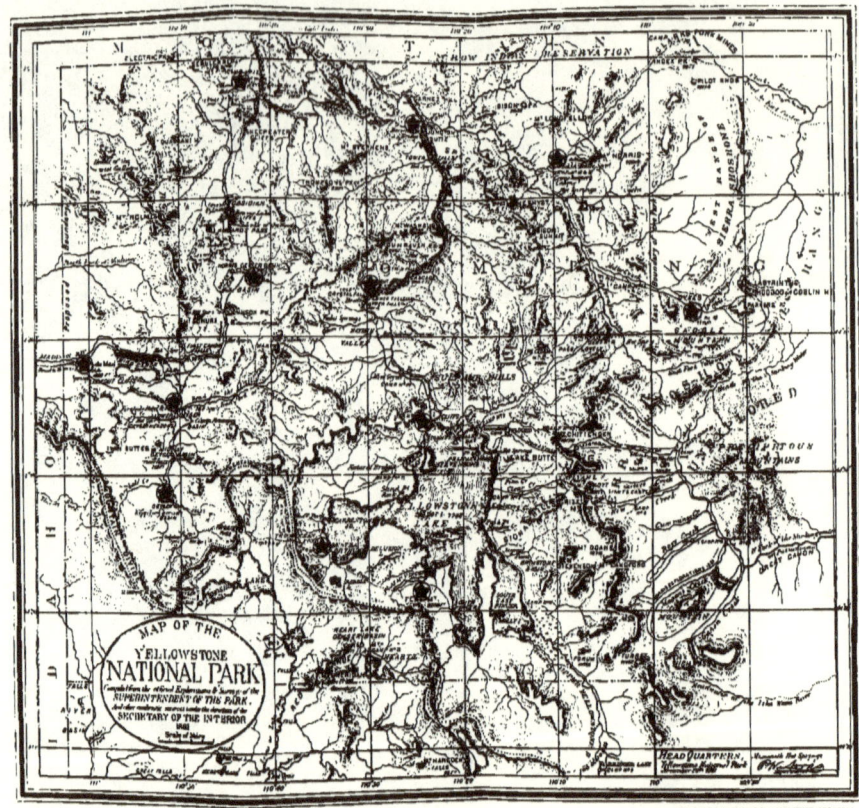

GUIDE-BOOK OF THE YELLOWSTONE NATIONAL PARK.

INTRODUCTION.

At the suggestion of some prominent and practical friends who have visited the Yellowstone National Park, or who propose doing so, I add a map thereof and brief description of its leading points of attraction, together with illustrations of some of those referred to in these legends, and a few practical suggestions regarding the season, the route, and the cost of visiting them. The map is a duplicate of that in my report of 1881, except the colors, and the size, which, in reducing to accord with the pages of this work, is somewhat small for clearness; but map, directions, and suggestions are considered at least as correct and practical as any yet published regarding the Wonder-Land.

PRELUDE.

In all these blooming valleys, along each crystal stream,
And snow-encircled lakelet, where quivering halos gleam,
These labyrinths of goblins, and spouting geysers grand,
Unnumbered are the marvels throughout the Wonder-Land;
As wintry storms build snow-fields, and summer breezes thaw,
All nature seems in contrast, in beauty, size, or awe,
Creation, growth, and *ruin*, the universal law!

LOCATION OF THE PARK.

From this map, in connection with that of the Land Office of the United States, it will be seen that the Snake River fork of the

Columbia, and Green River fork of the Colorado of the Gulf of California (Pacific waters), and nearly all the other great rivers of that part of the continent, including the Jefferson, Madison, and Gallatin forks, and the Big-horn and other branches of the Missouri, Mississippi (Atlantic waters), to a great extent radiate from spouting geysers or other hot springs within or adjacent to the great National Park, situated mainly in Wyoming Territory, and also embracing portions of Idaho and Montana.

This wonderful region is really less one large park than a group of smaller ones, partially or wholly isolated, upon both sides of the continental divide, which is much lower in the Park than the nearly unbroken surrounding mountain ranges. Its average altitude probably exceeds that of Yellowstone Lake, or nearly a half-mile higher than Mount Washington. Its few yawning, ever difficult, often impassable cañon approaches along foaming torrents, the superstitious awe inspired by the hissing springs, sulphur-basins, and spouting geysers, and the infrequent visits of the surrounding pagan Indians have combined to singularly delay the exploration of this truly mystic land.

Although Lewis and Clarke, by ascending the Jefferson instead of the Madison or Gallatin fork of the Missouri in 1805, crossed the Rocky Mountain divide west of the Park without its discovery, yet it is from a member of that early band of northwestern explorers that we derive our first knowledge of its existence.

Sergeant Coulter, after his honorable discharge from this expedition, and famous gantlet-running escape from the ferocious Blackfeet Indians, accompanied the Sheep-Eaters amid the spouting geysers, fire-hole basins, and other marvels of these regions, and ever after his return to Missouri in 1810 gloried in describing them; yet so little credence was given to his narrative that for many years, even long after I was first upon the Lower Yellowstone, Coulter's Hell was a standing camp-fire jest upon now well-known realities. But John Coulter was, without a shade of doubt, the first white explorer of any portion of the Yellowstone National Park.

The want of space prevents the use of much material at hand regarding the wanderings of Henry, Sublett, Bonneville, Bridger, and many other renowned trappers and Indian-fighters of those regions, of the fruitless United States exploring expedition of Captain Reynolds during 1859 and 1860 in search of the Park, or of the camp-fire legends of the gold-seeking pilgrims, some of whom, including Captain De Lacy, George Huston, G. H. Phelps, and Frederick Bottler, unquestionably visited portions of the Park prior to 1870, though none of them had then published narratives.

Having myself, long before the Reynolds expedition, failed, as he did, to reach the Park from the east, early in June, 1870, I again sought, after many years' absence from those regions, to reach it by ascending the Yellowstone above the Gate of the Mountains, accompanied by Frederick Bottler, from the Bottler ranch. Deep snows baffled our resolute efforts to cross the Madison range to the geysers, and, when seeking to descend to the Yellowstone Valley below the Mammoth Hot Springs, Bottler was swept away in attempting to cross a mountain torrent above Cinnabar Mountain, losing his rifle, ammunition, most of his clothing, and nearly his life. This mishap compelled our unwilling return from within the Park through the then nearly unknown and impassable second cañon of the Yellowstone to Bottler's, the only white ranchman at that time upon any portion of the mighty Yellowstone River. Thence I retraced my route to Fort Ellis, published a brief account of my trip (see No. 3 of my "Journal of Rambles in the Far West"), and, under previous engagements, descended the Columbia to the ocean, then proposing to return to the exploration of the Park the next year.

During the following autumn the Washburn expedition was suddenly organized for Park exploration. It was composed of H. D. Washburn, N. P. Langford, T. C. Everts, S. T. Hauser, C. Hedges, W. Trumbull, B. Stickney, W. C. Gillett, and J. Smith. General Washburn, in command, was then surveyor-general, T. C. Everts and N. P. Langford, ex-officers, and all prominent and esteemed citizens of Montana Territory. They were well equipped, and at Fort Ellis were joined by Lieutenant G. C. Doane and seven men. From here they followed my return route to and up the Yellowstone through its second cañon. They missed the Mammoth Hot Springs, but visited Mount Washburn, the Great Falls and Lake, returning by the Fire-Hole River and Madison route to Virginia City. When among the fingers of the Yellowstone Lake, Everts lost his way, horse, arms, and provisions, and after thirty-seven days of exposure, starvation, and suffering, doubtless unequalled by any other man now living, was found by Baronet and Pritchette, barely alive, upon the mountain which bears his name, near the Mammoth Hot Springs. This is the first party of really successful explorers of any considerable portion of the Park of which we have any public record.

The interest elicited by the publications of several of these parties led to Professor Hayden's geological explorations of 1871, and that to Congressional dedication, March 1, 1872, of the Yellowstone National Park, under the control of the Secretary of the Interior.

This laudable outburst of national enthusiasm in behalf of a peerless health- and pleasure-resort for our people seems to have subsided with its dedication; and, without any practical provision for its protection, it was for years abandoned to destructive forest-fires, wanton slaughter of its interesting and valuable animals, and constant and nearly irreparable vandalism of many of its prominent wonders. So uniform was the testimony of the civil and military officers of the government, as well as of the American and European scientists, and of myself and other tourists who visited the Park, and so strong their appeals to the nation for its protection, or at least the sending of a commissioner or an agent specially empowered to investigate and report the facts, that among the early acts of the Hon. Carl Schurz, Secretary of the Interior in 1877, was my appointment as superintendent of the Park, specially instructed to again visit it and report the facts as I should then find them, for the information of Congress; but as to funds for salary, or even expenses, none were furnished or promised, but I was left to rely upon Congress to make provision* for all salary and expenses prior to July 1, 1888, to properly pay for the performance of duties pointed out and positively required of the Secretary of the Interior in the act dedicating the Park.

Under these circumstances, and without pecuniary aid from any department, association, or individual, I proceeded, *via* Bismarck, Forts Buford and Keogh, the Custer battle-field, and Gate of the Mountains upon the Yellowstone, to the Park. After visiting the most important of its known wonders and exploring others, I started to descend the Yellowstone, but, meeting General Sherman, returned with him to Tower Falls. Here, by the breaking of a saddle-girth, I was unhorsed, and too seriously injured to proceed with the general or even to return home, except by descending the Yellowstone in a skiff from above the Gate of the Mountains, which course I adopted.

---

* This, upon the recommendation of the Honorable Secretary of the Interior and the endorsement of the President, unanimously passed both Houses since the close of my official connection with the Park.

During my return home the hostile Nez-Perces made a raid in the Park, which was so sudden and unexpected that General Sherman and his slender escort narrowly escaped capture. Several tourists, however, then in the Park, were killed, wounded, or captured. Among these was Professor Dietrich, whose body was riddled with bullets while he was standing in the door-way of the McCartney cabin at the Mammoth Hot Springs.

The facts and suggestions in reference to the Park, as submitted by myself to the Honorable Secretary of the Interior, were incorporated in his report of 1877 (part first, page 837), and also deemed by him worthy of publication in pamphlet form. (See Report of the Superintendent of the Yellowstone National Park for 1877.)

After a long and careful investigation of the whole subject, and in consideration of the written opinions of prominent scientists and explorers of our country, the cautious and prudent Congress of that period, at its first session, with flattering unanimity made an appropriation of ten thousand dollars for the protection and improvement of the Park, being the first ever furnished from any source, and with a portion of which the first improvements ever made in the Park were commenced at the Mammoth Hot Springs during the Bannock raid of 1878, and have been continued as appropriations have since been made.

AREA OF THE PARK.

Two matters in connection with the Yellowstone National Park tend to great and general misapprehension regarding it. These are, first, its name, and, second, its area, or, as perhaps best treated, inversely.

The United States maps and authorities show it to be an oblong square, 62 miles in length from north to south, and 54 miles in width from east to west, containing 3348 square miles.

The tenth census of the United States shows that the area of the State of Delaware is 1960 square miles; State of Rhode Island, 1085 square miles; District of Columbia, 60 square miles; and the aggregate area of the counties of New York, Kings, and Richmond, of the State of New York, is 150, equal to 3255 square miles. Thus the most recent and reliable authorities extant show that this great national land of wonders contains 93 square miles in excess of the aggregate area of two of the original thirteen States of the Union, the

District of Columbia, containing the capital, and the three counties of the State of New York, which embraces the commercial emporium of the first and third cities of the nation, having an aggregate population of about two million five hundred thousand. Nor is this a full statement of the case; as, if to this account were added the actual excess of surface measurements of this peculiarly broken region over those relatively level eastern ones, it would certainly exceed that of Connecticut, 4845 miles, and, with the adjacent Goblin-Land and other regions which I have explored during the past two seasons, fully equal that of New Jersey, Massachusetts, or several other of the original States of the Union.

This necessarily lengthy explanation of the first question as to the magnitude of the Park so nearly disposes of the second, as to the name, that I only add that, although it is so vast and broken by mountains and cañons into countless partially or wholly isolated parks and valleys, still the whole of it is nearly encircled by snowy mountains with few passes, being thus park-like in character, and the name correct, or at least difficult to substitute by one more appropriate.

The size and character of this work, together with the various poems and copious notes descriptive of many of the features and legends of the Wonder- and the Goblin-Lands, precludes extending the foregoing outlines of the Park, and hence I close this necessary prelude to our guide of routes with a few practical suggestions for those desirous of a charming ramble amid the countless marvels of this national heritage of wonders.

Neither the routes, modes of conveyance, nor hotel accommodations of the Park as yet equal those of our eastern homes, nor is it necessary or even desirable for the health or enjoyment of tourists, the most of whom in little groups of kindred or friends seek a season of variety and romantic privation in the snowy pass, the flowery park, or secluded glen of nature's unpolluted solitudes as a refuge from the duties of office, the dictates of fashion, or as a cheering, healthful solace from ceaseless toil or corroding care.

OUTFIT.

From long and trying border experience I can vouch that stimulants are not necessary but baneful,—buoyant hope and the azone of pure mountain air are matchless tonics and appetizers; but none who outfit themselves may fear to provide bountifully of tea, coffee, nutritious food, canned milk, and fruit, as well as warm, strong woollen clothing, blankets, shawls, etc., *and then double the outfit.* Few will regret relying upon *this* advice.

Heretofore it has been necessary to arrange before arrival for some reliable guide with tents, wagons, saddle- and pack-animals, and other outfit and provisions not brought by themselves. This, although perhaps judicious for those who have time and opportunity, is now less essential, as I learn that from Livingston, upon their main line, just below the Gate of the Mountains, a branch road will be completed through it and amid the enchanting scenery of the parks and canons of the Yellowstone, 50 miles to the mouth of the Gardiner, 4 miles below the Mammoth Hot Springs, and a hotel there, and elsewhere in the Park, in time for this season's rush of tourists.

The following letter from the General Passenger and Ticket Agent of the Northern Pacific Railroad Company gives all the facts that are obtainable at this date:

"NORTHERN PACIFIC RAILROAD COMPANY.
"GENERAL PASSENGER AND TICKET DEPARTMENT.

"ST. PAUL, MINN., April 12, 1883.

"P. W. NORRIS, Norris, Michigan.

"DEAR SIR,—Replying to yours of April 10, it is impossible to give the detailed information you desire regarding the accommodations in the Park at this early date. I can say approximately that the rate from St. Paul to the Mammoth Hot Springs will be ninety dollars for the round trip, and that the rates for transportation in the Park will be about twelve cents per mile. Our branch will be built and open to the Park about the 1st of July. A large force of men is now employed on the line building it.

"One large hotel will be built at the Mammoth Hot Springs, and smaller ones at Lower Geyser Basin, Upper Geyser, Great Falls, and Lake Outlet. Ponies, attendants, bath-houses, and appurtenances of like nature will be established in connection with the hotels and stage line.

"Yours, etc.,
"G. K. BARNES,
"*G. P. & T. A.*"

PROPER SEASON OF THE YEAR FOR A TOUR OF THE PARK.

The best of all months is August, then July, the first half of September, last half of June, the most of October and May, in the order named.

The fogs, rains, and floods from melting snows in early June, and the equinoctial snow-storm of September, are sure and fearful. July and August uniformly fine, the remainder of the year changeable, and successive seasons varying greatly.

No future danger from Indians or animals; no rattlesnakes or other venomous reptiles; gadflies often troublesome upon animals in June and July, but mosquitoes far less annoying than along the rivers *en route*.

TIME NECESSARY FOR A TRIP OF THE PARK.

This depends much upon the health, means, taste, and leisure of each person or party. A week of dash and jam in the Park will allow a glance at the main geyser-basins, Mammoth Hot Springs, Mount Washburn, Forks, Cañon, Falls and Lake of the Yellowstone, and other points of interest *en route*. Ten days are better, and fifteen ample for a fair tour of all the Park now opened up to roads and bridle-paths, while a mountain summer of three months can be most pleasantly and healthfully spent in the viewing and exploration of the Wonder- and Goblin-Lands for years to come, as between the Yellowstone Lake and the Big-horn River is one of the wildest, roughest, inaccessible, least known, and yet interesting regions of the United States.

COST OF A TRIP TO AND THROUGHOUT THE PARK.

This also, after leaving the railroad, is subject to variations similar to those of time, and dependent much upon them.

I have no information of essential change in the old rates of five dollars each for a guide and packer with his saddle-horse, or ten dollars for two men and their animals, and one dollar per day for each additional saddle- or pack-animal. The additional outfit, board, etc., if any, as the parties mutually agree, which, to avoid annoyance during the trip and at its close, should be clearly understood in writing before its commencement.

Should the mining developments of these mountain regions equal present indications, a railroad will reach the Park from the East *via* Clarke's Forks Mines or the Two-Ocean Pass, or both of them, as well as the Virginia City branch of the Utah Northern from Dillon within a few years hereafter, each road increasing accessibility and inviting a healthy competition for the patronage of tourists in making a cheap, rapid, and easy visit to the Wonder-Land; planning it as the turning-point, as well as the main region of attraction, in a season's ramble for health and enjoyment.

Should these anticipations be realized a visit to the Park will become national in character and popular with our people, so that ere long the flush of shame will tinge the cheeks of Americans who are obliged to acknowledge that they loiter along the antiquated paths to pigmy haunts of other lands before seeking health, pleasure, and the soul-expanding delights of a season's ramble amid the peerless snow- and cliff-encircled marvels of their own.

CHOICE OF LOOKOUTS.

Prominent among the bordering points of observation of this vast region is Electric Peak, near the northwestern border, elevation 11,775 feet; Mount Norris in the northeast, 10,019; Mounts Chittenden, Hoyt, Langford, Stephenson, and others in the eastern Sierra Shoshone border, and Mounts Holmes and Bell's Peak upon the western, ranging between 10,000 and 11,000 feet high, and Mount Sheridan, near the southern border, 10,385 feet high, still backed by the Grand Teton, landmark of all those mountain regions, which is over 13,000 feet in height. But Mount Washburn, towering upon the brink of the yawning Grand Cañon water-way of the Yellowstone Falls and Lake, 10,340 feet high, is the most central, accessible, and commanding for a general view of the Park and its surroundings. From its isolated summit can be plainly seen on a fair day, as upon an open map, not only this lake and cañon but many others also, countless flowery parks and valleys, misty sulphur and steaming geyser-basins, dark pine and fir-clad slopes, broken foot-hills, craggy cliffs, and snowy summits of the sundering and surrounding mountains. No tourist should fail in securing this enchanting view, the best plan of obtaining which is, upon reaching the meandering rivulet-fed lawns of the Cascade, the Glade or the Antelope Creeks, to go into camp and await the dawn of a cloudless summer's morning. Then to the scientist, the artist, or the poet, and to the weary and worn pilgrims of health and pleasure from our own and other lands, ardent to secure the acme of mountain-climbing enjoyment, or in viewing the lovely parks and yawning cañons, the crests of glistening ice and vales of blistering brimstone, the records of fire and flood, the evidences of marvellous eruptions and erosions of the present and the past, and day-dreams of the future in the commingling purgatory and paradise of the peerless Wonder-Land of earth, I would say leisurely ascend the terraced slopes of Mount Washburn, and from its oval summit, with throbbing heart but fearless eye and soul expanding, look around you. One day thus spent would more adequately impress the mind with the magnitude and marvels of the Park, and the vast amount of exploration and research necessary in finding routes, and the enormous amount of labor and hardship unavoidable in the construction of buildings, roads, bridle-paths, trails, and other improvements, even when unmolested by hostile Indians,—as during the past two years only,—than a perusal of all the reports and maps of the Park which have ever been published.

HEADQUARTERS OF THE PARK.

The loophole-turreted and triple-winged block-house Headquarters of the Park crowns the summit of an oblong grassy butte or hill 150 feet above the cedar grove, a portion of which, as shown in the illustration, is still standing, submerged and semi-fossilized by deposits from the mineral waters of the main active Mammoth Hot Springs, which rise in inimitably beautiful scollop-bordered pools and brilliantly-tinted pearly-white terraces directly fronting, and to an elevation greater than the balcony of the Headquarters. Thence through the shifting clouds of vapor ever escaping from these unique fountains, the active, the dying, the dead cedar-fringed and crumbling, then the dark pine and balsam-hidden pools and terraces rise successively as they recede to the most ancient and once powerful of the now extinct craters or cones upon the summit of the Terrace Mountain, which much of the year presents an outline of snow amid the clouds. Almost beneath this building, to the right, are seen the famous

Liberty-Cap crumbling cone of an extinct pulsating geyser, 45 feet high, the Devil's Thumb, somewhat smaller, numerous ragged-edged

MAMMOTH HOT SPRINGS.

pits of ancient pools, nearly as deep, the sinks of two cold-water creeks, the McCartney buildings upon, and the grassy slopes and craggy summits of the Sepulchre Mountain above them.

To the left the clear-cut sky-line of the White Cliffs, and eroded gorge of the West Gardiner just to the right, the pine-clad cone of Bunsen's Peak to its left, the yawning cañon and basaltic cliffs of the Middle Gardiner, and still farther to the left the nearly vertical walls and battlements above the double falls, and beyond them the silvery thread of the Cascades of the East Gardiner, with the Mount Stephens range in the background, are all in clear and undisturbed view. To the rear the descent is continuous and often terraced or precipitous for fully a mile to the Main Gardiner, and fine trout-fishing from the shelly geyserite roof of a subterranean river, to where its seething waters, in volume sufficient for a fine mill-stream, filled with the floating vegetation peculiar to these hot mineral streams, runs for some distance beside the cold snow-fed waters of the Gardiner before commingling. This is at the base of the nearly vertical walls of Mount Evarts, fully 2000 feet high, through a spur of which is a yawning water-way to the foaming Yellowstone near the Bear Gulch drainage of the gold and silver mines adjacent. (See notes 53 to 56.)

To this point ascends the road from the railroad below, and from it radiate those up the *East Gardiner* towards the forks and *falls of the Yellowstone,* that over the *Terrace Pass* to the *Geyser or Fire-Hole Basins* and *Yellowstone Lake,* and also a bridle-path between *Bunsen's Peak and the Falls of the Middle Gardiner,* via the Sheep-Eater cliffs to its junction with the Geyser road near Swan Lake.

MIDDLE GARDINER BRIDLE-PATH.

This bridle-path route offers at least one day of ramble among points of exceeding interest, and will be first described.

The route selected for a future road follows that now in use for hauling timber to its end; thence; *via* a cascade just below the impassable portion of the cañon of the West Gardiner; thence, deflecting to the left, ascends by a uniform grade along the timbered slopes of Bunsen's Peak to the present bridle-path below the falls of the Middle Gardiner. Along and between this route and the vertical White Cliffs, among the immense masses of upturned angular rocks there hurled from the cliffs, is one of the wildest thicket-hidden haunts of grouse, rabbits, and hares, as well as of bear, wolf, and wolverine, which I have ever visited, even afoot, in which way only the most of it can be traversed.

	Miles.	Miles.

The bridle-path, as now travelled, leaves this road near the edge of the timber, and crossing the deep valley of the West Gardiner, ascends steadily, sometimes steeply, near 2000 feet to the summit of the terrace between Bunsen's Peak and the yawning cañon of the Middle Gardiner, three miles from the Headquarters. 3

Near this point a trail blazed through the small pines and aspens leads within half a mile to Butler's Lookout, on the edge of a cliff rising fully 1000 feet from the winding thread of silver, about half a mile below the falls. This cliff, though at so great a distance and elevation from the falls, is the best point from which to obtain a good view of the nearly 200-feet leap, and also of the terrible cañon and looming cliffs of basalt, portions of which are uniquely radiate or fan-shaped.

Returning to the main bridle-path, and passing through alternate glade and grove for a mile, we reach the brink between the falls and the Sheep-Eater Cliffs, which extend a distance of 2 miles, in one portion of which they wall in a secluded lovely little haunt of the Sheep-Eater Indians, and hence the name and description at the time of its discovery. (See pages 10 and 11 of my report of 1879.) . . . 2 5

The trail skirts these cliffs less than a mile, and then through aspen groves and sedgy glades to its intersection of the Fire-Hole road south of Swan Lake, from which point it is about 6 miles by each route to the Headquarters 1 6

Bunsen's Peak can be ascended mainly upon horseback from the terrace of great sage-brush from the southwestern side.

In the dense thickets of small pines skirting the western foot of this peak are the decaying remains of an ancient drive-way of the Sheep-Eaters, and the ruins of one of their pole coverts for arrow-shooting is still standing just back of the verge of the cliff, a little southeasterly from the Rustic Falls. These are where the West Gardiner, after meandering through a grassy plain nearly to its border, glides some 40 or 50 feet down a mossy rock, so smooth, so placid, and so noiselessly as to present to one standing afoot or upon horseback, as can easily and safely be done upon its very margin of mist-nourished ferns and flowers, a contrast unique and matchless to the succeeding 1500 feet of dashing, foaming descent adown a ragged cañon water-way in magnitude immensely

too large for that now flowing there, and impassable for any but an experienced mountaineer afoot.
From these falls one may, by careful riding northerly within a mile, reach the summit of the Terrace Mountain, tread the terribly fractured verge of the White Cliffs, view the ancient cones of extinct geysers, obtain enchanting view of our valley, buildings, and the Mammoth Hot Springs at our feet, the snowy crests of Electric, Holmes's, and Bell's Peaks in the north and southwest, and also on a fair day the icy peaks of the Three Tetons, more than 100 miles away in the southern horizon. We thence descend northwesterly above and then through the Terrace Pass to the Headquarters. This trip, although so interesting, is one of only 10 or 12 miles in distance, a very easy day's ride, and can be made in much less.

ROAD TO THE GEYSER-BASINS.

	Miles.	Miles.
From the guide-board, near the Devil's Thumb, ascend the soft sinter terrace to the left, and by a winding way and some steep grades pass above, and overlooking the blue, active Hot Springs, and over or among the crumbling or forest-overgrown ancient cones and terraces to the summit of Terrace Pass .		2
Half a mile of slight descent, short turn to the left, and then through an open lawn-like valley, good water and camps to Swan Lake on the right .	3	5
Less than a mile back, a half-mile side trip to the left and sharp notch at the head of cañon, a good view of the Rustic Falls, Sheep-Eater covert on the cliff, and old camp of these Sheep-Eaters in the valley.		
Bridge over the Middle Gardiner	2½	7½
One mile above is the mouth of Indian Creek, which the hostile Bannocks descended from the pass between Holmes's and Bell's Peaks, and at their camp between the streams, just below, slaughtered a large number of captured horses for food in 1878. A fine ride of 5 miles and return will allow a good view of Bell's Peak, fine valleys and streams, *but no fish.*		
Cross and then ascend Obsidian Creek to the bridge at upper end of Willow Park, and first night's camp; water plentiful, but only passable; wood and grass abundant and excellent	3½	11
Opposite the lower end of some slide rock on the right		

	Miles.	Miles.
are two springs of ice-cold water, the last, except the indifferent water of the Lake of the Woods, which is palatable or safe to use for 5 miles . . .	1	12
Bridge and long causeway to Obsidian Cliffs and Beaver Lake	1	13
The grade between them was made by hurling dry pines from the cliff for eminence fires to fracture the huge blocks of native glass, and then pounding them down with sledges, in 1878. The best of the red, yellow, or banded specimens of obsidian are near the foot of the vertical cliff at the south end of the grade. Beaver Lake was made by these animals, whose dams and houses are still to be seen at various places upon it.		
The naked estuary-looking beach near the upper end of this lake is caused by poisonous water from *Green Creek*, which is to be seen at the right . . .	1	14
Long grade above a nauseous brimstone-basin on the right, then a fine view of Mount Holmes and Bell's Peak to the northwest from the drainage divide of the Yellowstone and Madison fork of the Missouri, then a slight descent to the Lake of the Woods, thus appropriately named at the time of its discovery, when I was searching for water which was not poisonous for one of my men, severely injured by the fall of his horse in a bear-fight	1	15
Several nauseous fire-holes to an open valley; good wood, water, and camps in the Norris Valley . .	2	17
Bridge over Norris fork and nearest camp to the Norris Geyser Basin	3	20
Uniquely beautiful blue Emerald Pool just to the left of the road on the second hill	1	21
The great cloud of steam to the left is from the New Crater, the outburst of which I witnessed, as shown in my report of 1878, which is now a powerful geyser of erratic habits and irregular periods of eruption of its column of waters, which is sometimes 100 feet high, but usually much less. At the foot of the hill beyond the Minute-Man, with regular spurts of 20 or 30 feet, and 200 yards south, in the foot of the hill, is the Monarch, which daily throws one vertical and two diagonal columns of hot water about 100 feet high, with rumblings which shake the valley, until a creek of hot water for a time bars all travel upon the road.		
The Vixen, Constant, and many others are very interesting, as also the finest plateau of boiling pools, and unique porcelain-like rims to funnels to be found		

	Miles.	Miles.

in the Park. The road could not be built through the middle of this basin, much of which, towards the northwest where I first discovered it in 1875, is still unexplored, and although one of the oldest, largest, and probably once powerful in the Park, for want of water or other cause has not now as many powerful geysers as the Upper Geyser Basin.

Through the balance of this basin upon the road, and a dense pine forest to a fine camp to the left of the mouth of the bubble-covered Geyser Creek . . | 3 | 24

This is one of the most charmingly secluded parks and camp of the mountains, and from the accessibility of the cascades and red pulsating geysers in the cañon of the Norris Fork 1½ miles above, the numerous lakes, the matchless Paint-Pots and geysers to the south, and the Monument Geyser Basin upon Mount Schurz to the west, must ever remain a favorite camping-place, the only drawback being the water, which, only palatable above, is utterly unfit for use below the mouth of Geyser Creek.

The only good water attainable is in the Gibbon, which is a cold, snow-fed stream from Mount Holmes to its confluence with the Norris fork, one mile above.

From this place we ran a wagon as far as possible with animals, then with men, towards the famous Geyser Cone, now in the National Museum in Washington, which was nearly two miles, by a circuitous route, to the foot of the bluffs beyond the Paint-Pots. There it required a blacksmith frequently sharpening tools, a man to assist in drilling and chiselling, and another to carry and throw cold water upon them to prevent parboiling in the hot steam and jets from its seventeen fine pulsating cones or orifices for nearly a week, and then twenty men to carry it amid the bottomless boiling chaldrons to the wagon, and thence it was conveyed safely to Washington, although weighing nearly half a ton.

A bridle-path extends from the end of this road through the earthquake shakes and fallen timber—11 miles in all—to Willow Creek Camp, upon the East Fire-Hole River; but it is unsafe to attempt to follow it without a guide.

In a horseshoe bend of the Gibbon, near the lower end of this park, we fortified our camp, while I explored the country, and we opened our road through the cañon of the Gibbon during the Bannock raid of 1878.

	Miles.	Miles.
Foot-bridge over the Gibbon at the head of the cañon	1	25
Ascent of Mount Schurz to the matchless cones and charming view from the Monument Geyser Basin and river, each 1–2.		
Two crossings of the Gibbon in its Grand Cañon, amid heavy boiling pools, and thence through open pine groves upon the plateau between the ancient channel of the Gibbon on the left, and its modern cañon torn through the spur of a mountain to the right to its 80-feet falls, many hundreds of feet below the road	4	29
Uniform descent to the old channel of the Gibbon at Cañon Creek	½	29½
Good water and fuel, but the only camp for miles is one-half mile up the creek before crossing, where wood and water are fine and abundant, but grass inferior in quality, ground boggy, and unsafe for picket-pins.		
Long grade, then open pine groves and burned tract to the Earthquake Cliffs	2½	32
The old road of 1878 passes below these cliffs to the Madison Cañon route.		
Dry, open route to the intersection with the old Madison Cañon road, and thence to Lookout Terrace, where we get the first view of the steam-clouds from the Excelsior and other geysers of the Fire-Hole Valley, stretching away to the blue foot-hills of the main Rocky Mountains just beyond the Upper Basin	2	34
Easy descent and fine road beside the broad grassy channel of the Madison; always full and seldom overflowed to its head at the confluence, or, as called, Forks of the Fire-Hole River; and thence to Prospect Point at the crossing of the East Fork	3	37
Near this point are now some rude government buildings, and from it roads diverge as follows:		

DILLON, ON THE NORTHERN UTAH RAILROAD, VIA HENRY'S LAKE AND VIRGINIA CITY, OR REVERSING THE ROUTE.

	Miles	Miles
Dillon to Virginia City, daily coach		65
Henry's Lake, hired conveyance, good fishing and camp	60	125
Riverside, within the Park, good fishing and camp	22	147

	Miles.	Miles.
Lookout Cliffs and lovely view of mountains and valleys	4	151
Marshall's Hotel, near the forks of the Fire-Holes	8	159
Excellent fords of both forks to Prospect Point	1	160
The route of 60 or 70 miles from Henry's Lake down its fork to Camas, or to Beaver Cañon, on the Northern Utah Railroad, is an old and natural one, but no inhabitants and little travelled.		

OLD MADISON CAÑON ROAD.

	Miles.	Miles.
Prospect Point to the mouth of the Gibbon, good camp and fishing		10
Five fords of the Madison in its cañon, good camp and fishing	6	16
Down the river to Riverside, good camp and fishing	3	19
From this point there is a somewhat shorter, newer, and rougher route down the Madison cañons to Virginia City.		

QUEEN'S LAUNDRY ROAD.

This was opened and our camp made at the foot of the Northern Cliffs to the Geyser Meadows, from which, by a steep bridle-path, we reached our line of road, while constructing it amid the old snow-fields on the Madison Plateau to the Lookout Cliffs, late in July, 1880.

It was while thus engaged that, during a Sabbath's rest and bathing recreation, some of the boys crossed from our camp to the attractive bordered pools below this great boiling fountain, and in one cool enough for bathing discovered its matchless cleansing properties, and from the long lines of bright-colored clothing soon seen drying upon the adjacent stumps and branches, while their owners were gambolling like dolphins in the pools, the envious cooks and other camp *attachés* dubbed it the Laundry, with a variety of prefixes, of which that which I deemed the most appropriate adheres, and hence the name Queen's Laundry 3

Thus from Prospect Point it is a six-, and from Marshall's Hotel four-mile trip, through lovely groves and glades, and amid unique geyser and other hot-spring cones to visit and, by a bath-house which I constructed in 1881, or hopefully a better one, test for themselves the velvety feel and cleansing properties of these waters.

A road from this spring through lovely parks and groves *via* the accessible Twin Buttes, as near the 200-feet Fairy Falls as the bogs below it will allow, and thence to the Midway Geyser Basin, so that tourists might go one route and return the other in a visit to the Upper Geyser Basin, is one of the routes planned and blazed out, but not completed, before my leaving the Park.

GEYSER VALLEY ROAD.

During the summer and early autumn this road is usually, though portions of it not always, a good one.

	Miles.	Miles.
It will be remembered that from the Headquarters to Prospect Point is		37
Thence to old Camp Reunion, near the butte to the left, *short*	1	38
It was here that a portion of the Hayden expedition of 1878, under Gannitt and Holmes, and some of Wilson's soon after, set afoot by the hostile Bannocks near Henry's Lake, and my own party, after many weeks of travelling from different directions, first met white men, and rudely fortified a camp for concentration while variously engaged in exploration, geological research, and construction of our road up the main Fire-Hole River.		
White sinter in the Lower Geyser Basin to a laminated plateau on the left, where are several interesting pools and geysers, the most regular and best known of which is the Fountain	1	39
Plain of white sinter, or geyserite, a creek and several rivulets of hot water, then to the right of the main road is the rocky ford of the Fire-Hole River, just below the Excelsior Geyser, where its deluge of seething water, cloud of scalding steam, or shower of hot rocks do not prevent its use	2	41

On page 58 of my report of 1881 is a sketch by Hayden, in 1871, of this geyser before it was known to be one, but frequently called "Hill's Half-Acre," and on page 62 a sketch by myself in 1881, after one season's eruptions, and a reliable narrative of all then known of it, from which I briefly quote in substance that its first known eruption somewhat retarded the return of our wagon in 1878, its constantly increasing agitation and discharge of hot water until its commencement of eruptions in February, 1881, as a daily geyser, and after various spasmodic changes " seems to be settling down to business as

	Miles.	Miles.

a regular two- or three-hour intermittent geyser, but so immensely excelling any other ancient or modern known to history that I find but one name fitting, and hence christen it the Excelsior until scientists, if able, shall invent one more appropriate." The crater of this volcanic geyser has been immensely increased, the timber along the river for some distance below it killed, the ford and the camp opposite rendered unsafe, and the cloud-capped pillar of vapor arising therefrom, even when not in eruption, become so great and peculiar as to have been a clear-cut and unmistakable landmark from nearly every mountain-peak in all my explorations of the entire Sierra Shoshone, and portions of the Yellowstone, Madison, and Rocky Mountain Ranges during 1881. There is a great scallop-bordered pool or lakelet of deep-blue hot water on a self-formed plateau just above, and others about the Excelsior, the steaming, foaming hot-water outlets of which are bordered by brightly tinted, pearly formations too delicately beautiful for pencil to paint or pen portray.

The main road to the end of the river, and that across the Geyser plateau, unite after the latter has, by a rapid rocky ford, crossed the river and passed through a group of interesting ancient pools and spasmodic salses 1   42

The road thence winds along the low foot-hills, sandy terraces, and marshy meadows of the Fire-Hole River to a rocky ford between the Fan and Riverside Geysers, and thence, as shown upon the map of the Upper Geyser Basin, to Old Faithful, the most reliable of all known geysers, at the head of the basin, which our wagon, the first that ever made a track up the main Fire-Hole Valley, reached on the 29th day of August, 1878 5   47

As this map shows the relative location and the table of geysers,—the character of the eruptions of the most prominent of them,—I will here only insert an illustration of the Bee-Hive Geyser in eruption, and quote pages 20 and 21 of my report of 1880 as descriptive of the usual phenomena of geysers.

SPOUTING OR INTERMITTENT GEYSERS.

Without attempting to decide a mooted question among savants as to the true origin of these prominent wonders of the Park, I venture to state that successive years of careful observation tend toward the

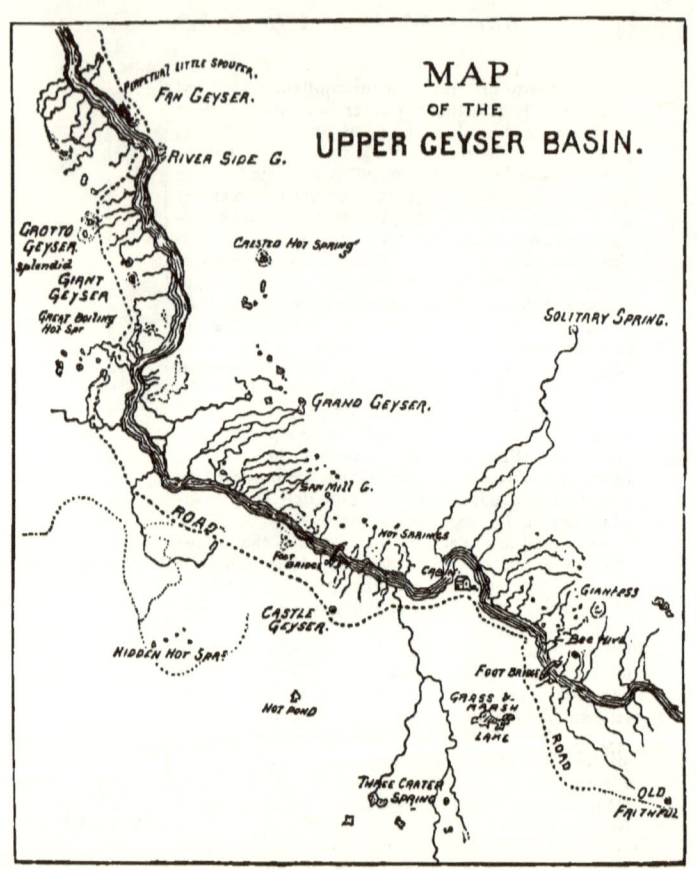

theory that, like pulsating geysers, salses, fumeroles, and most of the other kinds of hot springs, they are primarily escape-vents for the earth's pent-up internal fires. In these vents the chemical action of escaping gas and high-pressure steam produced by contact of this escaping gas-heat with the permeating surface-water, by dissolving the wall-rock increases the heat and enlarges the orifice of these small, tortuous, and otherwise cooling fissure-vents.

Slow, but sure and constant, change attends them all, and many, though probably not all of them, at the proper stage become true intermittent spouting geysers. This can occur only when the orifice is so nicely adjusted in height, size, and form to the power of the escaping steam and gas in the self-formed chamber beneath, that the pressure of accumulating water for a time nearly or quite prevents its escape except through sympathetic fumeroles or natural safety-valves. But the constantly-increasing force from beneath ultimately overpowers the pressure of the water, when, after more or less subterranean rumbling, earth trembling, and sundry kinds of bubbling, gurgling, and spluttering, the aqueous monster seems fairly aroused, and then occurs the grand eruption. This is usually through one, but occasionally through several circular or oblong vents, cones, or craters, with diverse kinds of throttlings and pulsations in the different geysers, each having its own peculiarities in color and size and in the shape of the orifices, as also in the height, power, and direction of the column or columns of water and the length of the periods of eruption and of repose; and even these, as above stated, are doubtless slowly changing.

While the foregoing theory seemingly accounts for the usual manifestations of geyser eruptions, still the rending of huge geyser cones and the hurling of tons of rock, as have occurred at the Giant and New Crater Geysers and elsewhere, seem to indicate an occasional outburst of some greater power. Explosions of superheated steam or of gas, misplacement of the safety-valve upon escape-vents of internal fires, infernal regions, or other places of pent-up power are occasionally suggested by phenomena otherwise inexplicable.

To the Upper, Lower, and Midway Geyser Basins upon the Fire-Hole Rivers, and others less important upon the shores of the Yellowstone, Heart, and Shoshone Lakes, early discovered by others, my own explorations have added the Monument, the Norris, and the Paint-Pool Basins upon the Gibbon or its branches, the Safety-Valve

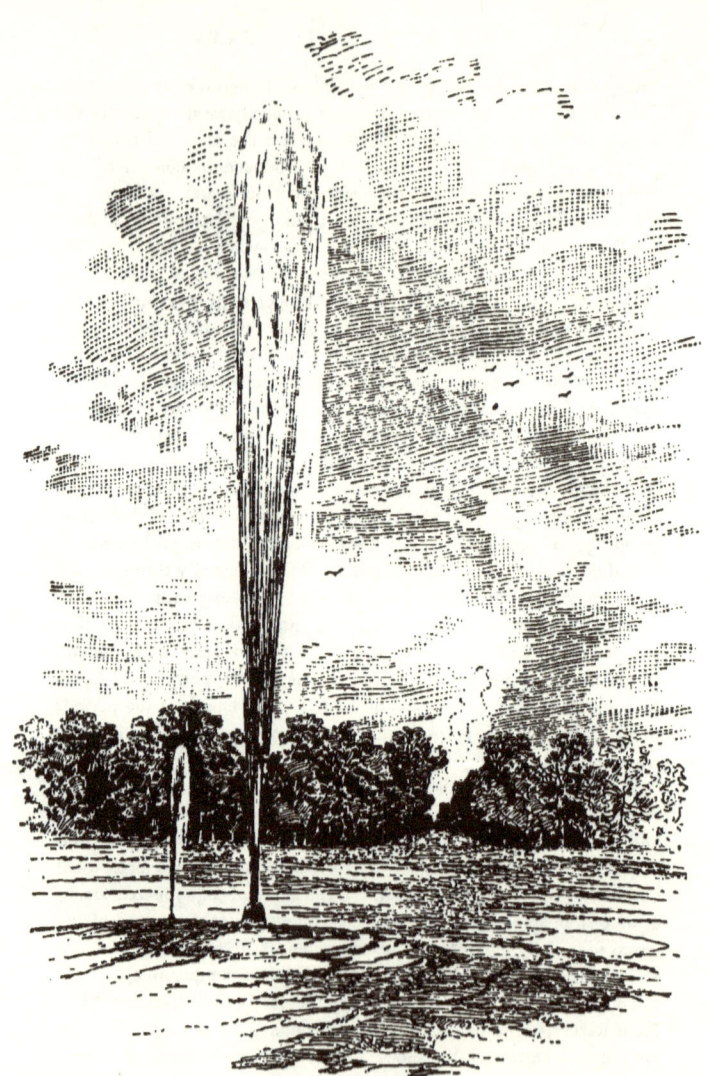

BEE-HIVE GEYSER.

in the Grand Cañon of the Yellowstone, and several others, less important, in other portions of the Park, which is now so well explored that there seems little probability of additional *basins* of importance being hereafter discovered. Still, as my own explorations have mainly been made in connection with the ever-urgent duties of exploring or opening roads or trail routes, and the scientific explorers of the Park have labored under many and grave disadvantages during brief periods of summer only, amid hostile Indians, doubtless interesting isolated geysers, or perhaps small groups of them, may yet be discovered. In fact, so little, comparatively, is yet known of the number, size, and peculiarities of the various geysers or other springs of these regions that I deem it one of the most inviting fields for further scientific investigation.

ERUPTIONS OF SPOUTING GEYSERS.

Although, as above shown, each class of geysers has its own peculiarities and approximately regular periods of eruption, yet of Old Faithful, which alone of all the large geysers has no fumerole, escape-vents, or sympathetic geyser, and a few others with small ones are they as yet known, and hence until a more careful and continuous observance of them I view any table of eruptions more as an indication when to look for, rather than when to rely upon seeing a full eruption, notably from those having long periods of repose, sympathetic geysers, or even nature's safety-valves,—fumeroles.

UPPER GEYSER BASIN.

Name.	Periods of Eruption.	Continuance of Eruption.	Height of Column.	Remarks.
Old Faithful...	A trifle less than 1 hour.	3 to 5 minutes.	125 to 180 feet.	No fumerole or sympathetic geyser.
Bee-Hive...	Each 24 hours.	3 to 4 "	175 to 225 "	One small fumerole, which spouts a little first. This also sometimes has a smaller eruption daily.
Giantess...	Approximately each week.	2 to 6 hours.	100 to 250 "	Several sympathetic pools, frequent spoutings, but seldom a full one.
Castle...	Daily or oftener.	15 to 60 minutes.	25 to 50 "	Seems short of water, and when supplied spouts much higher.
Grand...	Daily or oftener.	Several 3-minute spasms.	100 to 200 "	Turban and other escape-vents.
Giant...	Unknown.	6 or 8 hours.	100 to 300 "	Several fumeroles now; geysers which usually, but not always, prevent a full eruption.
Splendid...	Each 3 or 4 hours.	3 to 5 minutes.	125 to 175 "	Similar to Old Faithful, only more spreading.
Grotto...	Each 4 or 5 hours.	5 to 10 "	25 to 40 "	Several orifices; very beautiful.
Excelsior...	Each 3 or 4 hours.	3 to 5 minutes.	50 to 300 feet.	So much steam as to much hide the water.

MIDWAY BASIN.

LOWER GEYSER BASIN.

| Fountain... | Each day or oftener. | 5 to 15 minutes. | 50 to 100 feet. | Several others near, probably sympathetic. |

NORRIS BASIN.

Monarch...	Daily.	20 to 40 minutes.	60 to 100 feet.	Three orifices at once; an immense amount of water.
New Crater...	Daily, and another hourly.	3 or 4 "	30 to 50 "	In constant agitation, but the heavy eruptions irregular.
Minute-Man...	Each minute.	10 seconds.	25 to 35 "	Diagonally and spout-like.

	Miles.	Miles.
Leaving the bridle-path to Shoshone and Yellowstone Lakes for the present, we return to Prospect Point. .	10	57

ROAD TO THE YELLOWSTONE LAKE AND FALLS.

This passes through the old war-path gap just south of Prospect Point, in a mile pass where the tourist Cowan and family were captured by the Nez-Perces in 1877, then in the open valley of the East Fire-Hole River, and over several good fords to Rocky Fork, fringed by willows, but fine water, grass, fuel, and camp, but no fish . . . . 5 | 62

Open valley past the dangerous trail to Gibbon Meadows to our old camp to the left on Willow Creek . 2 | 64

A wild mountain route, which I often took up this stream, and through a timbered pass alive with game to the Fire-Hole on Alum Creek, beyond the mountain, before grading the road up its face; should not be attempted by any but a good mountaineer or accompanied by a reliable guide. Cross a marsh, and then meander, steadily rising to the long but excellent grade up the face of the mountain, and thence along an ancient dry cañon outlet of Mary's Lake to its fine beach and clear but brackish waters. No fish and poor camp . . . . 4 | 68

In the open pines of the summit, just east of this lake, is the remains of Chief Joseph's corral in 1877.

Down amidst the foaming springs, scratching fumeroles, and scorching brimstone-pits of the Alum Creek Fire-Hole Basin we descend to a sheltered grassy camp on a small branch entering from the right. Tepid water, but fine fuel, grass, and sheltered camp . . . . 3 | 71

The oft-repeated and published assertion that there are no fish upon this route between the Mammoth Hot Springs and the Yellowstone River is somewhat incorrect, as they are sparsely found at some seasons of the year in the lower Gibbon and head of the Madison; and in the branch above this camp and others east of it there are abundance of game trout just above where they join the sour hot waters of Alum Creek, which would pucker a persimmon or scald a Nevada lizard. I do not attempt to account for the presence of these trout here, or their absence in waters apparently more favorable for them to reach or inhabit, as I am not advancing

	Miles.	Miles.

theories, but recording facts for the guidance of others.

From this camp the road cros es enchanting pine- and balsam-bordered parks, winds through a region of eroded and still eroding buttes, and then makes nearly a direct stretch over the treeless valley of Sage Creek to the old trail near the Yellowstone River . . . . 7 | 78

Here the road forks, and taking that to the right, we find a good road along the open terraces of the enchanting Yellowstone, descend a steep grade near a rocky rapid, and among the numerous bubbling, spluttering pools of the famous Mud Volcanoes to the open valley near the corral of Chief Joseph. To the left fine camp . . . . 2 | 80

A little farther to the left, on the eastern margin of the main Mud Volcano, is what vandals have spared of the rudely-constructed defences of this chieftain's headquarters while his people were crossing at the best ford upon the entire Yellowstone River below the lake.

This is at an island half a mile above, and should not be attempted without a guide; but trout, large, handsome, and gamy, without number, and, from the countless long white worms with which they are infested, without value, unless to persons as hungry as we have sometimes become, when they prove neither unpalatable or unwholesome.

At some rude stone-heaps beyond and to the right is the camp of General Miles after his Clark's fork defeat of the Bannocks in 1878, and a winding road through lovely groves and grassy lawns, and skirting the truly "Peerless Lovely River," we descend a slope to a grove and matchless camp at the foot of the mystic Yellowstone Lake . . . . . 6 | 86

From this camp or the long sand-spit below it I have often crossed the river with a raft, swimming the horses, to the trail to Concretion Cove, which starts out from the beach nearly a half-mile up and through the dense timber to the muddy fords of the Pelican, is a difficult trail to follow.

As it may be desirable for many parties to divide at the Upper Geyser Basin, and while one outfit proceeds with wagons along the road we have just traversed to the end of it, at the lovely camp and site for a hotel and steamboat-landing at Toppin's Point, just above, the other, with saddle- and pack-train, come by the mountain trail, which we now re-

| | Miles. | Miles. |

turn to trace. It will be remembered that from the Mammoth Hot Springs to the Upper Geyser is called in miles 47
This is much less than estimated by us when constructing or by others in traversing it; and although the results are similar in the odometer measurements of Captain Stanton and Lieutenant Steever, under the orders of General Sheridan, in 1871, throughout the Park, still, as being the only semblance of measurements ever made of our roads, I adopt them, not as positively, but as approximately correct.
From Old Faithful we take the bridle-path through a fine open pine forest across a rocky ford of the Fire-Hole River, old Geyser Basin, along the steep cliffs and some boggy rivulets upon it, to the magnificent cascades which, from the intrepid twelve-year-old son of Governor Hoyt, of Wyoming, who unflinchingly shared in all the hardships, privations, and dangers of the explorations of his father and the lamented Colonel Mason in 1881, in which they passed them, I felt justified in calling Kepler's Cascades. They possess wild romantic interest, well worthy of a trip from the Upper Geyser Basin by those who return from there 2 49
Thence the trail winds through a rolling timbered region and a valley skirting the nearly vertical walls of the continental divide to a sharp turn to the right and slight ascent in a narrow rocky cañon and the boggy, swamp-bordered summit pond or marsh, within 2 miles, cuts directly through the Rocky Mountains, and without warning reaches the brow of the cliff overlooking the De Lacy fountain-head of that branch of the Snake River fork of the Columbia River 6 55
This is the low, direct, and short but muddy Norris Pass, thus named by the famous scout and guide, Yellowstone Kelly, upon its discovery by myself, after fruitless search by himself and others for any pass in that vicinity. The descent of 400 or 500 feet is steep, even for pack-animals, but neither rocky nor boggy to the De Lacey camp, in one of the most secluded and charming parks in the mountains 1 56
A lovely side ride 2 miles to the deep snow-fed waters of the Shoshone Lake, with its beach glistening with shiny particles of obsidian, but no fish, nor is there any in Lewis Lake, 4 miles below; while Heart Lake, 7 miles beyond, and many other adja-

cent lakes and ponds, seemingly no different saving boggier shores, are literally filled with them of different varieties. Many of the young pines among those storm-strewn in this region are dotted or literally covered with unique bulgy knots, which when cut and peeled in summer form fine walking-cane souvenirs. The somewhat interesting geyser-basins at the head of this lake are too remote and inaccessible to justify a visit by any but scientists.

By steep winding, but neither muddy nor precipitous ascent through a pine forest again brings us to the summit of the Rocky Mountains at Two-Ocean Pond 3½   59½

From one or two rocky points above the timber a charming view may be had of the Yellowstone Lake, sleeping in matchless beauty at our feet, with the evergreen-clad terraced sides and snowy summits of the Sierra Shoshone Range towering amid the clouds beyond. The descent is winding, steep, and log-obstructed to the hot-spring camp at the western end of the Great Thumb of Yellowstone Lake . 3   62½

For an explanation of the name of this and other portions of this famous lake, as well as of its peculiar contour, reference is made to note 32; and for a brief statement as to the catching and broiling of the large, wormy trout along this geyserite beach, see note 36.

This hot-spring beach is the point from which to make the side trip to Mount Sheridan and Heart Lake upon the Pacific drainage, through dense and often tangled or fallen pines and parks, but without a vestige of a mountain on the continental divide, which is here the levellest stretch of land in the region, and one of the least elevated.

Distance to Mount Sheridan (unless that dashing officer opened a route last summer) anywhere from 10 to 20 miles; time, 2 days; outfit, *extraordinary*,—a full supply of tough clothing, and *stanch* fortitude to prevent wear and tear of flesh, and also of conscience, for imprecations at the pines, the packers, the saddle- and pack-animals, and above all the person who advised making this side trip. A renewal of this outfit will be necessary for those returning *via* the Upper Yellowstone, Two-Ocean Pass, and Wind River route, that of the Stinking-Water, or even the eastern shore of the Yellowstone Lake to its foot.

From the fishing-camp our bridle-path or trail traverses a fire-hole basin, crosses a high bluff, and reaches a

	Miles.	Miles.
hot creek and poor camp in a forest too dense for safety in picketing horses	6½	69
Rough route through annoying fallen timber 5 miles, sharp turn to the left, and from a bold ridge the first and best view of the arch of the Natural Bridge is had at a distance of fully a mile northwesterly, which we reach by winding to the left over a warm-spring creek and possible camp.		
Though not one of the leading points of attraction, it is the best near it, and a substantial, natural roadway over a small stream, over which a great game-trail passed, and I shot a fine grizzly in ambush among the fallen timber at its western abutment at my first visit, which was alone; but the accurate description of the bridge to be found on pages 22 and 23 of my report of 1880 is too long for copying here . .	6	75
Romantic ride through groves and parks to the foot of the lake	5	80
Description of the trails beyond the lake and river will be deferred.		

ROAD TO THE YELLOWSTONE FALLS.

Retrace our route to the crossing of Sage Creek (at the lake, 86)	8	94
Deep valley and rounded, grassy hills to the Sulphur Mountain, which is uniquely interesting, but soon seen, and from sulphur fumes and poison water a poor camp	1½	95½
Fine road over a treeless plain to Allen Creek . .	1½	97
The broad, bare estuary appearance of the borders of this stream is due to the sour mineral properties of its waters below, where they are hot, similar to which is Sour Creek, which enters the Yellowstone nearly opposite.		
Crossing a treeless terrace, a long dugway in the side of a mountain, and skirting the broad, placid waters of the river to the cove near the rapids, one-fourth of a mile above the Upper Falls . . .	3	100
This is the present end of the road from this direction, there being a gap of 16 miles by one bridle-path and 18 by the other to Tower Falls, where the road from the Mammoth Hot Springs now terminates. It is at this camp that, breast-high upon a pine-tree about 20 inches in diameter, are still legible upon the bark, "J. O. R., Aug. 29, 1819," which is the oldest record by white man of which I have any knowledge in the Park. Upon the banks of the		

	Miles.	Miles.

creek, with a broad mouth, about a mile above this, are the old brands of the slaughtered tourist's camp-fire referred to in the poem "Lonely Glen" and note thereto.

The broad, tranquil river here rapidly converges, as its current increases, to the narrowest point upon the river below the lake, which is scant 70 feet, where the abutments of a bridge are commenced over the foaming rapids at the head of the Upper Falls. These, in a half-cascade leap of about the same as the Falls of Niagara, reach the again broad channel, so shallow and gliding that, at the proper stage of water at least, Yellowstone Kelly and myself have forded it upon horseback just above the mouth of the Cascade Creek. (See note 71.)

Within the distance of about one mile from the camp, in the cove above the main rapids, we skirt them to the Upper Falls upon the bridge, as illustrated, across the Cascade Creek (see note 81) and falls, and reach the camp at the head of the trail (not bridle-path) to the Great Falls of the Yellowstone .	1	101

Descent to the head of the falls 500 feet, where on the pole-railed shelf amid the mist the nearly 400 feet of clear leap, the narrow thread of foaming water, and the brightly-tinted walls of mighty eroded cañon are beside, beneath, or before you, and to the right, opposite, and above, at my favorite camp, when able to cross the river above to reach it, is far the finest location for a future hotel to be found in the vicinity.

From the camp above the Great Falls one bridle-path follows the verge of the Grand Cañon to the right, another through the open sage-brush plateau to some fine camps within a mile on Spring Creek and to the left.

THE MOUNT WASHBURN BRIDLE-PATH.

Open, grassy ridge, and descent to a large and fine camp on Cascade Creek above its cañon. (See notes 68 and 69.)		2
Open, occasionally boggy valley, then skirt Dun Raven's Peak to the left, and the main peak of Mount Washburn upon the right, to a grassy plateau, from which an easy and safe ascent of less than one mile brings us to the oval summit	7	9
Long grassy slope to forks of the trails . . .	4	13
Rolling open hills 1 mile, then continuous descent to camp at Tower Creek above the falls . . .	2	15

GRAND CAÑON BRIDLE-PATH.

	Miles.	Miles.

Skirting the brink of the Grand Cañon from the camp above the head of the Great Falls of the Yellowstone to Lookout Point . . . . . . | 1 | 102

This rudely railed rocky cliff directly fronting the Great Falls, and 1000 feet nearly vertically above the foaming rapids in the Grand Cañon below them, is far the best point for an unobstructed view of them all, than which few places earthly combine as much of the unique, the beautiful, and the grand.

The two notches observable in the brink of the Great Fall were first noticed in the spring of 1881, when a heavy slide of rocks at the cleft of Spring Creek, past the Red Pinnacles, where the famous artist Bierstadt took one of his sketches of the Great Falls the same season, also destroyed the route of descent to the foot of the falls. (See note 70.)

Upon the opposite side of the Grand Cañon, a mile or so below Lookout Point, is the shelf of rock from which the great artist Moran made one of the sketches for his famous painting of the Falls of the Yellowstone, now in the upper anteroom to the Senate chamber in Washington. Below this point, upon that side of the cañon is the Sliding Cascade, 1400 feet high, nearly opposite to which the bridle-path leaves the cañon for the meadow camp, which is good, but poor water . . . . . | 3 | 105

PAINTED CLIFF BRIDLE-PATH.

From the lower end of the meadow to the right, 1 mile through open pine forests, another steep descent to the small but beautiful Safety-Valve Geyser, and another constant descent through an ancient fire-hole brings us to good trout and trout-fishing at the uniquely beautiful Painted Cliffs, nearly 2000 vertical feet below our meadow camp, and the only place where a trail reaches the river between the Great Falls of the Yellowstone and those of Tower Creek.

Open, sometimes boggy, meadow, pine forest, Fire-Hole Basin, with a black-mud geyser on the left, to the charming secluded camp of Glade Creek . . | 3 | 108

Long and, in portions, rocky ascent to the summit of Rowland's Pass of the upper spur of Mount Washburn, for a description of which, and its discovery, reference is made to the note to "In Cabin, Camp, or Council." (See note 87.) . . . . | 2½ | 110½

GUIDE-BOOK OF THE PARK. 267

	Miles.	Miles.
From the brushy summit of this pass there is a fine lookout a few rods to the right, and within half a mile beyond another, commanding a fair view of the yawning Grand Cañon above and below, as well as those of the Broad and Orange Creeks beyond it. To the left the route (not well opened) of a good bridle-path to the snowy summit of this spur of Mount Washburn and a magnificent view of all the surrounding regions, second only to that of the highest peak, which can be reached during much of the summer by a romantic ride or walk of less than 2 miles along the crest of this spur. The descent from Rowland's Pass is continuous, but not steep, along the grassy slope of another spur to the clear icy waters, luxuriant grass, and abundant fuel of the finest groups of charming sheltered camps in the mountains, at the crossings of the snow-fed rivulet-feeders of Antelope Creek, nearly west from the ancient ruin of unknown builders mentioned in my reports, but now burned . . .	2½	113
Romantic undulating valley, brilliant with flowers, to the forks of the bridle-paths	3	116
TOWER CREEK AND FALLS.	2	118
Good camp on Antelope Creek to the right; best place for a view of the wonderful Tower Falls a little down the creek; thence a steep descent to its confluence with the Yellowstone, beneath vertical walls many hundreds of feet in height, ornamented and capped by the long horizontal lines of remarkably beautiful basaltic columns. The old Indian ford of the Yellowstone, just above, is dangerous, but the nauseous gas from the adjacent springs is not, nor does it affect the waters of these streams, in each of which, near their confluence, are trout and trout-fishing unsurpassed in the mountains. A steep, continuous ascent of 500 feet from the bridge above the falls brings us to the summit of the cliff and wagon-road from the Mammoth Hot Springs. From this peculiar point of attraction the road passes through open groves of huge fir-trees, resembling eastern hemlocks, some steep descents and cañons to Hot-Spring Creek, and camp just above the famous Baronet's Bridge at the forks of the Yellowstone	3	121
Less than 2 miles nearly west from this camp is a		

	Miles.	Miles.
small lake, and along the steep cliffs to the right, as well as on the slope of a side branch below it to the north, are the stumps, from 2 to 15 or 20 feet high, of fossilized ancient trees still erect, and many fallen, and a fine place to secure beautiful fragments, as well as chalcedony, agate, amethyst, and other formations found in them or strewn along the cliff or creek.		
Hot-Spring Creek, past forks of Miners' trail, to fine camp in Pleasant Valley	2	123
Much steep grade, but several good camps, to the summit of the Devil's Cut, or Dry Cañon . .	2	125
Upon the bald patches of the eroding basaltic terraces to the left of this cañon are countless unique geodes filled with various beautifully-tinted crystals and concretions; grassy slopes and terraces to the dark cliffs of the modern lava-beds to the left, and a yawning cañon to the right; fair camp . . .	4	129
Grassy pass and plains to bridge over Black-tail Deer Creek	2	131
Grassy valley and terraces to the Upper Falls of the East Gardiner River, 40 feet high	3	134
Beneath the dark foliage of the trees at the eastern end of the rustic bridge at the brink of these falls may still be seen some of the boughs of my rude couch, made as related in note 75.		
From this place the ascent is easy from across the bridge to a wild region along the towering cliffs of the Gardiners, and to the right those of Mount Evarts. From the brink of the cliffs north of these falls, and nearly in the spray of another, where one can pass between the sheet of water and wall-rock, there is a charming view of the long grade of our road adown the cañon of the East Gardiner, our headquarter buildings, the mist-clouds and white terraces of the Mammoth Hot Springs, clear-cut upon the green slopes of the Sepulchre Mountain, which we reach at	4	138

MINERS' BRIDLE-PATH FROM THE FORKS OF THE YELLOWSTONE TO THE SODA BUTTE MEDICINAL SPRINGS.

Baronet's Bridge is upon the site of the first one ever built upon any portion of the Yellowstone, and the scene of many thrilling scenes, some of which are referred to in the poem and attached note of "Oh, is there in this World so drear?"

Open route and valley past a dark lava butte on the

	Miles.	Miles.
right, two lakes filled with water-fowl on the left to Amethyst Creek	1	10

From this creek there are several steep but not difficult routes of ascent to the grassy dome south, which is the front and lower one of the famous Specimen, or Amethyst Mountain, from the fossilized trunks and stumps of ancient forests upon which, the first, the greatest number and among the finest specimens of fossil wood, chalcedony, onyx, opal, and beautifully-tinted agates, amethysts, and other crystals ever found in any region have been obtained, and comparatively few, obtainable without heavy work with pick and fuse, remain. But those with curiosity, nerve, and a good horse can follow near the verge of the cliffs about a mile, and then descend, zigzagging their horse as I have done, to our old camp in the aspens, beneath in the valley to the left, or go the whole 2 miles along the cliffs, descending by the timbered cañon beyond. They will find descent a vertical half-mile at either of these places is not boy's play.

	Miles.	Miles.
The valley route is smooth and open, affording a fine view at a half mile's distance of the countless fossils, stumps, trunks supported by the vertical walls or the prostrate logs of a succession of ancient forests, the roots of one often over the tops of that beneath to a vertical height of nearly a half-mile; to the east fork of the Yellowstone	2	12
Here the bridle-path forks, and following that to the left in the open valley and across the creek, we reach the famous ancient geyser cone and present medicinal springs of Soda Butte.	3	15

This is the legendary spring of the surrounding Indian nations for the cure of the saddle-galls of horse, or arrow or other wounds of warriors, and besides properties similar to those of the Arkansas Hot Springs, will soon fatten man or animal using it. To this add its location in a sheltered valley amid and in plain view of the fossil forests and basaltic snow-capped cliffs of the Specimen, Longfellow, Norris, Grand Tower, and other surrounding mountains, it cannot (properly managed) fail of soon becoming one of the foremost summer resorts of the continent.

CLARK'S FORK MINERS' TRAIL.

	Miles.	Miles.
From the Soda Butte this bridle-path passes the famous Trout Lake	2	17

23*

270   GUIDE-BOOK OF THE PARK.

	Miles.	Miles.
Round Prairie	3	20
Line of Montana	4	24
Cook City, in the centre of a wonderful group of gold and silver lodes, not developed, but of great promise	3	27

Thence there is a bridle-path, *via* the base of the Index Peak and Heart Mountain, to the Stinking-Water Valleys, one fork of it to the Big-horn Valley and Fort Custer, and the left-hand one, near Clark's Fork Cañon, to the plains, and thence to Coulson, upon the Northern Pacific Railroad, whence I learn there is a purpose of running a line of travel, but I doubt it being properly opened this season, and will ever be a wild, elevated, romantic route for trail, road, or railroad.

GOBLIN-LAND BRIDLE-PATH.

Half a mile southeasterly from the crossing of the east fork, on the Miners' route, is the Gamekeeper's Cabin, built by Harry Yount, the famous scout and guide of Wyoming, while my assistant, as gamekeeper of the Park, and where he spent the winter of 1880 and 1881.

From this cabin the bridle-path traverses the open, grassy slope of Mount Norris to the ford of Cache Creek,—thus named by a party of forty odd gold-seeking pilgrims who were there set afoot by the Indians and cacheing,—*i.e.*, burying what they could subsequently find and not carry off,—by the aid of a pair of donkeys who would not go with the Indians, made their return afoot in 1864		3
Through groves and glades up the east side of the east fork to Calfee's Creek	4	7
East Fork Valley, and over a steep bluff to the left, on to Miller's Creek	2	9
North or left-hand bluffs of Miller's Creek to its forks	8	17
Zigzag ascent of 1500 feet, and then through open parks and dense thickets among the snow-fields to our old camp near the group of deserted Indian teepees and lodges at the foot of Parker's Peak .	5	22
Down a yawning cañon to the Goblins on the left .	2	24
Ascent of the Hood's Mountain to our monument of 1880	1	25

From the illustration (see page 43) of a portion of these Goblins, those in my report of 1880, and description of this region when first explored in 1880 and 1881 (see note 87), some conception can be formed of them; but only actual view can ever fully impress the mind with the weird, unearthly character of the dykes, cañons, and goblins of one of the wildest regions which I have ever seen in all my mountain wanderings, although the peaks and cañons are on a much grander scale along the Sierra Shoshone Range to the south.

We were kept in our old camp amid the balsams during the 4th and 5th days of September, 1881, by a howling storm, which broke away, so that C. M. Stephens and myself waded through deep snow to the summit of the Goblin Mountain, and spent the entire day of the 6th shivering beside our instruments in fogs from melting snow in the cañons, through shifting rifts, in which we got what bearings were possible under the circumstances.

Renewal of the storm in all its fury drove us to the Soda Butte Valley (below it) on the 7th without making our proposed exploration of less than 20 miles through a terribly broken region to the Fort Custer trail, whence, from near Crandle Creek, I think a route may be found to the Goblin Mountain. Two miles above our trail, on Cache Creek, are some interesting hot medicinal springs, and countless fine trout in the waters still discolored by them.

FOSSIL FOREST BRIDLE-PATH.

	Miles.	Miles.
From Gamekeeper's Cabin to the foot of Amethyst Mountain, nearly opposite a fire-hole in the foot of Mount Norris		3
Summit of Amethyst Mountain	3	6
Orange Creek and camp	5	11
Sulphur Hills	4	15
Forks of Pelican Creek	8	23
Indian Pond and Concretion Cove, on Yellowstone Lake (camp.)	5	28
Lower ford of Pelican Creek	3	31
Yellowstone Lake, half a mile above the foot	3	34

These distances—estimates only—and the route from fallen timber difficult without a guide.

NEZ-PERCE BRIDLE-PATH.

Indian Pond to Pelican Creek Valley		3
Upper ford of Pelican Creek	3	6
Nez Perce ford of the Yellowstone	6	12

Good route with a good guide, and difficult in many places without one.

CONCRETION COVE AND INDIAN POND.

One of the loveliest camps in the Rocky Mountains, and where the unique concretions figured and described in my reports, and referred to in my poem and notes of the "Mystic Lake of Wonder-Land," are plentifully found.

There are no really good fords, and few of any kind on the lower Pelican, but these birds and other water-fowl, as well as wormy trout, are plentiful beyond conception.

PASSAMARIA, OR STINKING-WATER BRIDLE-PATH.

	Miles.	Miles.
Concretion Cove to Turbid Lake		3
Jones's Pass of the Sierra Shoshone Range . .	7	10
Confluence of the Passamaria and Stinking-Water .	12	22

A rough route, elevated pass, and thence a fearful cañon above the forks of the Stinking-Water.

RECAPITULATION OF DISTANCES, ROADS, BRIDLE-PATHS, AND TRAILS WITHIN THE PARK.

ROADS.

Road to the Geyser-Basins.

	Miles.	Miles.
Mammoth Hot Springs to Terrace Pass		2
Swan Lake Camp	3	5
Middle Gardiner Camp	2½	7½
Willow Park, good camp	3½	11
Cold Springs	1	12
Obsidian Cliffs	1	13
Green Creek, poison water	1	14
Lake of the Woods	1	15
Norris Valley, good camps	2	17
Norris Fork, good camps	3	20
Norris Geyser Basin	1	21
Geyser Creek, good camp	3	24
Foot-Bridge to Monument Geysers	1	25
Falls of the Gibbon	4	29
Cañon Creek, half-mile below camp	½	29½
Earthquake Cliffs	2½	32
Lookout Terrace	2	34
Prospect Point, near the forks of the Fire-Holes Camp	3	37
Lower Geyser Basin	2	39
Excelsior Geyser, Midway Basin Camp	2	41
Old Faithful, Upper Geyser Basin Camp	6	47
Return to Prospect Point	10	57

Road to Henry's Lake, Virginia City, and Dillon, on the Utah Northern Railroad.

Prospect Point to Marshall's Hotel		1
Lookout Cliffs	8	9
Riverside, camp and trout	4	13
Henry's Lake	22	35
Henry's Fork, route to the Utah Northern R. R. at Camas, 65		
Virginia City	60	95
Dillon, coach daily to railroad	65	160

Old Madison Cañon Road.

Forks of Roads		4
Mouth of Gibbon, camp and trout	5	9
Foot of Madison Cañon, camp and trout	6	15
Riverside, camp and trout	3	18

Queen's Laundry Road.

To the Bath-Rooms		3/6
Return	3	6

Road to the Yellowstone Lake and Falls.

From Mammoth Hot Springs via the Upper Basin		57
Rocky Fork Camp	5	62
Willow Camp	2	64
Mary's Lake, brackish water	4	68
Alum Creek Camp, and trout near	3	71
Sage Creek, forks of road, and wormy trout; *no wood*	7	78
Mud Geysers, good camp, wormy trout	2	80

	Miles.	Miles.
Foot of Yellowstone Lake	6	86
Return to Sage Creek	8	94
Sulphur Mountain	1½	95½
Mouth of Alum Creek Camp, wormy trout	1½	97
Cove above the Upper Falls Camp, wormy trout	3	100

Bridle-Path to Tower Falls.

Crystal Falls, short half-mile	½	100½
Great Falls, short half-mile	½	101
Lookout Point, camp half-mile north	1	102
Meadow Camp, passable water	3	105
Painted Cliff Trail and return, 6		
Glade Creek, fine camp	3	108
Rowland's Pass (ascend Mount Washburn 2 miles)	2½	110½
Antelope Creek, splendid camp	2½	113
Forks of Bridle-Paths	3	116
Tower Creek, good camp, fine trout	2	118

Mammoth Hot Spring Road.

Hot Spring Creek, or Forks of the Yellowstone, good camp and trout	3	121
Pleasant Valley, good camp	2	123
Dry Cañon	2	125
Lava-Beds, several camps	4	129
Blacktail Deer Creek and camp	2	131
Upper Falls of the East Gardiner	3	134
Cascades of the East Gardiner, half-mile above		
Mammoth Hot Springs	4	138

Middle Gardiner Bridle-Path.

Mammoth Hot Springs to the Falls of the Middle Gardiner		3
Sheep-Eater Cliffs	2	5
Road to the Geysers	1	6

Shoshone Lake Bridle-Path.

Kepler's Cascades		2
Norris Pass of the Rocky Mountains	6	8
De Lacy's Creek and Camp, Pacific waters	1	9
Two-Ocean Pond, summit of the Rocky Mountains	3½	12½
Thumb of the Yellowstone Lake, camp	3	15½
Hot Spring Creek, poor camp	6½	22
Natural Bridge, near camps	6	28
Foot of Yellowstone Lake, camp	5	33

Mount Washburn Bridle-Path.

Great Falls of the Yellowstone to Cascade Creek Camp		2
Spur of Mount Washburn, which ascend 1 mile	7	9
Forks of Bridle-Paths	4	13
Tower Falls Camp	2	15

Painted Cliff Bridle-Path.

Meadow Camp to head of Grand Cañon		1
Safety-Valve Pulsating Geyser	1	2
Yellowstone River at Painted Cliffs	1	3

Paint-Pots Bridle-Path.

	Miles.	Miles.
Mouth of Geyser Creek to the Paint-Pots		1
Geyser Gorge	1	2
Earthquake Gorge	2	4
Rocky Fork Crossing	2	6
Mary's Lake Road, near Willow Creek	5	11

Miners' Bridle-Path.

	Miles.	Miles.
Baronet's Bridge, at Forks of the Yellowstone River		
Amethyst Creek, camp and trout		10
Crossing, East Fork of Yellowstone River, camp and trout	2	12
Soda Butte, Medicinal Springs, camp and trout	3	15
Trout Lake	2	17
Round Prairie	3	20
North line of Wyoming	4	24
Clarke's Forks Pass Camp, near northeast corner of the Park	3	27

Hoodoo, or Goblin Mountain Bridle-Path.

	Miles.	Miles.
Gamekeeper's Cabin, on the Soda Butte, to Hot Sulphur Springs		2
Ford of Cache Creek	1	3
Alum Springs and return	4	7
Calfee Creek	4	11
Miller's Creek	2	13
Mountain Terrace	8	21
Old Camp	5	26
Goblin Labyrinths	2	28
Monument on Hoodoo or Goblin Mountain	1	29

Fossil Forest Bridle-Path.

	Miles.	Miles.
Summit of Amethyst Mountain		3
Gamekeeper's Cabin to foot of mountain	3	6
Orange Creek	5	11
Sulphur Hills	4	15
Forks of Pelican Creek	8	23
Indian Pond at Concretion Cove of the Yellowstone Lake	5	28
Lower Ford of Pelican Creek	3	31
Foot of the Yellowstone Lake	3	34

Passamaria, or Stinking-Water Bridle-Path.

	Miles.	Miles.
Concretion Cove to Turbid Lake		3
Jones's Pass of the Sierra Shoshone Range	7	10
Confluence of the Jones and Stinking-Water Fork of the Passamaria River	12	22

Nez-Perce Bridle-Path.

	Miles.	Miles.
Indian Pond to Pelican Valley		3
Ford of Pelican Creek	3	6
Nez-Perce Ford of the Yellowstone	6	12

THE END.

www.ingramcontent.com/pod-product-compliance
Lightning Source LLC
Chambersburg PA
CBHW031935230426
43672CB00010B/1928